MEDITATIONS

A Collection of Weekly & Holiday Reflections

DONNA JUNKER

GREEN WINE
FAMILY BOOKS

MEDITATIONS: A Collection of Weekly & Holiday Reflections
Copyright © 2018 by Donna Kasik Junker
Library of Congress Control Number: 2018958058
    Junker, Donna Kasik, 1961 —
    ISBN 978-1-935434-94-8
Subject Codes and Description:
    1: REL012070 Religion: Christian Life-Personal Growth 2: SEL019000 Self-Help: Meditation 3: REL077000 Religion: Faith

Cover design by Brian Lane Green

Printed in Australia, Brazil, France, Germany, Italy, Poland, Spain, UK, and USA   Also available on Espresso Book Machine and anywhere good books are sold.

The Press does not have ownership of the contents of a book; this is the author's work and the author owns the copyright. All theory, concepts, constructs, and perspectives are those of the author and not necessarily the Press. They are presented for open and free discussion of the issues involved. All comments and feedback should be directed to the Email: [comments4author@aol.com] and the comments will be forwarded to the author for response.

Order books from www.gea-books.com/bookstore/ or the author at donnajunker@roadrunner.com or any place good books are sold.

Published by
GreenWine Family Books
A division of
GlobalEdAdvancePRESS

Old Testament verses are taken from The New Oxford Annotated Bible New Revised Version, Edited by Bruce M. Metzger and Roland E. Murphy, New York: Oxford University Press, 1994.

New Testament verses are taken from The EVERGREEN Devotional New Testament (EDNT) - Community and Family Education Edition (C.A.F.E.), By Hollis L. Green, Nashville. Post-Gutenberg Books, GlobalEdAdvancePRESS. 2015, unless noted.

DEDICATION

This book is dedicated to my family,
who fill my life with joy:

My husband Paul

My son Joshua and his wife Sharon

My grandchildren Chloe and Cameron

Meditations: A Collection of Weekly and Holiday Reflections is a multifaceted journey that the author hopes will contribute to the reader's ability to see their Faith in a new light. The meditations can be followed in order or chosen at random according to what is going on in the life of the reader. Enjoy the adventure!

CONTENTS

Introductory Thoughts

DANGER!

By Scott Gunn

Terrorist attacks in the United States might leave some of us feeling especially afraid. People of faith might be tempted to think of the church as a place to flee, to escape the scary world. But I don't think this is the right impulse.

Not long ago, I was at St. Bart's Church in New York City for a meeting, and a few of us wandered through their beautiful church a bit before we started. It so happens that some work is being done on their magnificent pipe organ, and they had put up some caution tape. "Danger!"

Every church should require a danger sign, for the Gospel is not meant to be comfortable! The Gospel requires this kind of warning.

You see, the Gospel is dangerous. There's nothing whatsoever that's safe about being a disciple of Jesus in this earthly life. There's a reason Jesus and others in the scriptures are always saying, "Be not afraid!" We are meant to be secure in God's love for us, but we are also meant to be out in the world sharing God's love in extravagant, even dangerous, ways.

My friend who serves as a priest in Europe said this the day after a Catholic priest was murdered during mass in his own church, "Today we open wide the doors of our church, because that is what we do." He has it right. Christians who serve as missionaries in dangerous places have it right. Congregations who care more about mission than maintenance have it right. Leaders who welcome change instead of clinging to the status quo have it right. Fire and police chaplains who run toward burning buildings have it right. Bold risks and brave actions are the stuff of the Gospel. Safety and comfort are not.

To be sure, it is understandable that we'd be afraid. I lock my doors at night. I keep a wary eye out when I'm walking alone. I get worried when I watch the news sometimes. But to all these situations, Jesus responds, "Be not afraid."

The Christian's place is wherever people need to hear a message of hope and love. Followers of Jesus will reject attempts to peddle fear for its own sake. When churches are beacons of grace and love, rather than comfortable museums, the Bible says, "There is no fear in love, but perfect love casts out fear; for fear has to do with punishment, and whoever fears has not reached perfection in love" (1 John 4:18). We are humans, so we'll never manage to reach perfection. We'll always have a bit of fear with us, which is why we need those danger signs. The signs remind us to expect a bit of fear. But we can, if we allow God to work in our lives, be defined by hope and love, not hatred and fear.

The church needs a warning, because just when we might want to linger in safety and shirk our duty, the Gospel demands that we look out to where there is great need.

Be not afraid! It's easier said than done. But by God's grace, we can be people in whom love casts out fear.

Scott Gunn is an Episcopal priest and serves as executive director of Forward Movement. He is co-author of *Faithful Questions: Exploring the Way with Jesus.*

Peace

There once was a king who offered a prize to the artist who could capture the perfect description of "peace" in a painting. Many artists submitted paintings, but there were only two paintings the king considered that he thought reflected peace. One painting was a calm lake. The water was as still as glass, which mirrored the beautiful majestic mountains all around. The sky was a beautiful blue, bright sunshine, dotted with puffy white clouds; this painting was a perfect reflection of calm and peace. The other painting also had mountains, but unlike the other picture, these mountains were brown, rugged and bare. The sky overhead was gray and ominous, filled with storm clouds and rain, and there was a rushing waterfall in the background. Nature was not calm and peaceful at all in this particular painting. However, behind the waterfall was a tiny bush jutting out of a crack in a rock. In the bush was a small bird nest, and in the midst of the rush of angry water, sat a mother bird on her nest – in perfect peace.

Guess which painting the king chose to win the contest of depicting perfect peace? The second one. Why did he choose that one? Because he said that, "Peace does not mean to be in a place where there is no noise, trouble or hard work. Peace means to be in the midst of those things and still be calm in heart…"

Jesus said, "*These things I have spoken, that in Me you might have peace. In the world you will have tribulation, but be of good cheer: I have overcome the world!*" (John 16:33). Of course we know there is a great deal of trouble, noise, and persecution in this world, but like the mother bird who built her nest in the midst of the turmoil, we can rest in the peace of God no matter where we are or what we are going through. Jesus also said, *"Peace I leave with you; My peace I give to you: but not as the world gives. Let not your life be troubled, neither fearful"* (John 14:27). Jesus spoke those words of peace to His disciples shortly before He was abandoned by His friends, tortured, and put to death for the sins of the world.

The apostle Paul experienced great hardships throughout his ministry, including beatings, stoning's, prison, deprivation, and isolation; yet, he was still able to write to the Philippian's, *"Be anxious for nothing; but under all circumstances by general prayer and specific petition joined with thanksgiving let your personal needs be made known to God. And the authentic peace of God which transcends all comprehension shall guard your hearts and your minds through Christ Jesus"* (Philippians 4:6-7).

In this coming New Year, no matter what it brings, may we be like the mother bird in the painting, and rest in the mighty hand of God's perfect peace.

(Credit given to Rev. Dennis Stueve, President of the Lutheran Braille Workers – story adapted from his winter 2016 LBW newsletter)

Led By God

Epiphany is a Christian festival, observed on January 6, commemorating the manifestation of Christ to the gentiles in the persons of the Magi, the wise men who followed the Star to visit baby Jesus. The word Epiphany is from Koine Greek ἐπιφάνεια, *epiphaneia*, meaning "manifestation" or "*appearance.*" It falls on the twelfth day after Christmas, and for some denominations, it signals the conclusion of the Christmas season. The Magi were probably astronomers who may have taken up to two years to find the Christ-Child. The Bible does not state how long their journey lasted, but it does state that they entered the house (Matthew 2:11) of Mary and Joseph to see Jesus, so we know they were no longer in the stable where He was born, as most movies depict. The Gospel of Matthew, chapter 2:1-12 is the only place in Scripture that mentions the Magi. Because they brought three gifts: gold, frankincense and myrrh, tradition has said there were three of these wise men, but we do not know that for certain.

Could you imagine following a star to find some very specific location? What if someone asked where your house was located, and you told them to follow some very bright star to find you; do you think they could do so? Could you? Surely God was helping to lead the Magi to Jesus. When these wise men left on their journey, they had no idea specifically where they were going or exactly how long it would take them, yet they went because of a deep desire to see this new King. God created this longing in the Magi, which He continues to create in us today. God still leads us today to His Son, just as He did over 2000 years ago. Are we open to following His lead, even if it takes us to places unknown, for an indeterminate amount of time? Do we press on as the wise men did, believing God is guiding us and having the faith that He will bring us to the exact place He wants us to be, even when we are unsure?

When the Magi arrived, they not only brought gifts, but they worshipped; we too must worship in the presence of the Son. The wise men brought gold, which is a very precious metal, symbolizing the Kingship of Jesus. Gold was a symbol of divinity (God in the flesh) of which overlaid the Ark of the Covenant (Exodus 25:10-17). Frankincense represented Jesus' priestly role. It is highly fragrant when burned, and was used in worship as a pleasant offering to God (Exodus 30:34). Myrrh symbolizes the eventual death and resurrection of Jesus. Myrrh was used as an anointing oil (Exodus 30:22-33) as a spice used in embalming, and was also an incense used at funerals. Myrrh was sometimes mixed with wine, such as what may have been given to Jesus on the Cross.

What gifts do we bring to Jesus, not once a year, but daily? He wants the gift of ourselves: our love, our obedience, our worship, and our very lives. Do we see Jesus as our King, sacred and precious, as our Priest, who we worship, and our ultimate Sacrifice for sin who loves us beyond comprehension? When we humble ourselves before God, He will give us a desire to find Him, and He will lead us to His mercy and grace, and take us places we never imagined; when we get there, like the Magi, we will be in awe of Him.

The Sacredness of Life

One of my favorite movies is, "*It's a Wonderful Life*." I watch this movie every year on New Year's Eve or Day. It is an old movie (made in 1946) about a man named George Bailey who was having tremendous difficulties in life, and whose entire life did not turn out at all as he had hoped and planned. George always wanted to get a college education, travel the world, do "great" things, build cities, remain "free" and single, have money, and live a life of adventure. Instead, George was never able to go to college; he did get married, had several children, was poor, and never had the opportunity to travel. When his life completely fell apart, in his desperation, he planned to kill himself; however, an angel named Clarence was sent down to earth from Heaven to protect George and save him. George told Clarence that he wished he had never been born, so the angel made that a realty. Miraculously, through this angel, George was then given the chance to see how life would have been if indeed he had never been born.

When George was about twelve years old, he saved his younger brother Harry from drowning when he fell in a frozen pond. Later in life, Harry saved hundreds of men during World War II as a fighter pilot. Had George not been born, his brother, Harry, would not have saved all of those men during World War II. George also made Mary, his wife, very happy, and gave her several children, all of whom would not have been born if George was never born. George's mother was widowed, but found great joy in her grandchildren – a joy she would have been robbed of if George was not alive to have them. George earned his living working at a Savings and Loan and helped many people live in nice homes, even when they could not really afford to, because George was so patient and generous. The movie relays how these people would have lived in the slums of the richest man in town, Mr. Potter, if George was not there to help them. The basic premise of the story is how important each person's life is, and the impact each life makes on the lives of so many people. In the end, despite living a very different life than he planned, George realized how truly blessed he was and just what a wonderful life he did indeed have.

There has now been over forty years of legalized abortion in this country. I realize that this is a very sensitive subject, but I only wish to view it in the light of Scripture and in the reality of my own life and the awesome mercy and forgiveness of God. I was a single mom at age 19. My son's father said he "was not ready to be a husband and father" and left our lives shortly after he heard I was pregnant – never to be seen again except for a few times when my son was a baby. I received no support from him of any kind. I had no education, no money, and after my son was born I worked two and three jobs at a time to support us. We were very poor, and my life's plans did not turn out as I had hoped either, just like George Bailey in the movie. It would not be until I was 30 years old that I could afford the time and money to go to college, graduate school and seminary (which all took a very long time, attending part time while working full time), but I know that my son's life has touched many people's lives, that he has brought people to Christ, and that God has worked wonderful things through him. Also, one of my greatest joys in life is being a mom and a grandmother – something I never would have been if my son was not born.

Scripture says we are *"fearfully and wonderfully made"* and that God's, *"eyes saw my unformed body"* when I was *"woven together" in my mother's womb. "All the days ordained for me were written in Your Book before one of them came to be"* (Psalm

139). Isaiah 49:1&5 says, *"The Lord called me from the womb, from the body of my mother He named my name... He formed me from the womb to be His servant.* Each life that is conceived is planned by God for His purposes. May we not interfere with the plans and purposes of God, and may we value each life, born and unborn, knowing that each life will in turn touch so many other lives.

The Golden Mean

Most people are afraid of something – fear of pain, fear of death, fear of heights, fear of the dark, fear of the unknown, fear of failing, fear of public speaking; the list can go on and on. Where does fear fit in when it comes to our faith? Is there any room for fear? As human beings, can we ever live without any fears? The ancient Greek philosopher Aristotle spoke about what he called, the "Golden Mean," which is a concept about finding a middle ground *between* extremes. For example, when we think about fear, we can be reckless and have no fear at all, or at the other end of the spectrum, we can be paralyzed with fear and live in terror, which is incapacitating. The middle ground, or the Golden Mean, is a healthy in-between place, where we might experience a normal fear, but we are not terrified. An example of this Golden Mean is when I took sky diving lessons. If I was terrified, I would have never jumped out of the plane. On the other hand, if I had no fear whatsoever, I might carelessly omit all of the safety checks that are necessary for a successful and safe jump.

In January, we celebrate Martin Luther King Day, and for good reason. Rev. Dr. Martin Luther King Jr. lived by his faith, perhaps with some normal human fears; but, because of his faith, he lived with more courage than most of us. His powerful leadership enabled others to push aside some of their fears as well for a just and godly cause. During the Civil Rights movement, when Dr. King saw the injustices that occurred to the black American population (especially in the South), his faith trumped his fears. Dr. King realized that God is ultimately in control, not us, and that God is a just God who created all men and women equally. But Dr. King was killed for his fearless work, right? Yes. God never promised that NO sparrow would fall to the ground, He simply promised He will always be there and is in control when one does fall. Luke 12:4-7 says, *"Be not be afraid of those who can kill the body, and then can do no more. But be forewarned whom you should fear: Fear Him, who after death has the power to cast you into hell; Yes, I say, Fear Him. Are not five sparrows sold for a penny, and not one is forgotten by God? Even the hairs of your head are all numbered. Fear not then: you are more valuable than many sparrows."*

Isaiah 41:10 says, *"So do not fear, for I am with you; do not be dismayed, for I am your God. I will strengthen you and help you; I will uphold you with my righteous right hand."* The right hand of God denotes power, which God has over all the universe. The enemy wants to make us fearful so we will not be fruitful. Imagine if Dr. King let fear get the best of him? God gave us His armor which we can wear to "battle" in this world. Ephesians 6:10-17 explains how God gives us all that we need to fight. Prayer and the Word of God, through our faith, will win our battles and overcome our fears.

God is the only one who is ultimately in control anyway – not us. Like a child, when we are dependent on God, we do not have to be afraid. Colossians 1:17 says, *"He (God) existed before all things, and by Him all are sustained and held together."* God is always in control, and He is still on the throne! He may allow us to suffer or even fall like the sparrow, but as 1 Peter 1:6-7 says, *"Herein you are triumphant, even if it is presently necessary to be saddened by trials of many sorts, this must be so you can give proof of your faith, a more precious thing than gold tested by fire, this proof will bring you praise, and glory, and honor when Jesus Christ is revealed."*

Dr. King and many others in the Civil Rights movement did indeed suffer, and like a sparrow, the leader of the Civil

Rights movement did indeed fall. However, his courage and his faith opened the eyes of a blinded nation to the justice and righteousness of God, who created all people equally in His image. May we celebrate Dr. King's legacy in the faith that God truly does consider us "*worth more than many sparrows*." God will equip us with all that we need to face our human fears in this life, and may we realize that He is constantly watching over us.

Wasted Lives

Who wants to live a meaningless, wasted, inconsequential life? I think all people would say they do not, but how many of us in fact do waste our lives, or much of them? What is the meaning and purpose of your life? How do you spend your time? What do you devote yourself to, and why? What is your passion in life? Is your focus in life on what makes you happy and comfortable, or do you prefer to get out of your comfort zone and serve God in whatever way He calls you? The Bible says, *"Do you not know that your body is a temple of the Holy Spirit which is in you, which you have of God, and you are not your own? For a great price was paid to ransom you: therefore, honor God with your body"* (1 Corinthians 6:19-20). The price we were bought with was a heavy price – the life of Jesus.

Our focus needs to be on what God wants us to do in this life, why He even created us and gave us life, and to serve and follow Him completely. Our primary focus should never be on our own comforts and happiness. John Piper (Chancellor, pastor, teacher, and author) wrote a book entitled, "Don't Waste Your Life." He wrote, "I will tell you what a tragedy is. I will show you how to waste your life. Consider the story from the February 1998 Reader's Digest: A couple 'took early retirement from their jobs in the Northeast five years ago when he was 59 and she was 51. Now they live in Punta Gorda, Florida, where they cruise on their 30 foot trawler, play softball and collect shells…' Picture them before Christ at the great Day of Judgment: 'Look Lord. See my shells.' That is a tragedy." According to John Piper, a tragedy is living a wasted or inconsequential life, which he defined as a life lived for self and for one's pleasures only – a shallow life. We are given one life on this earth which is meant to glorify God, to serve Him, and to love and serve others. That does not mean that we cannot find pleasure, fun, and relaxation in life, but that should not be our sole pursuit in life.

In the book mentioned above, Piper recalled his father, who was a pastor, sitting in a pew with an old man, who had finally accepted Christ. The man cried in that pew and said, "I've wasted my life;" those words haunted Piper for years. As a former hospice chaplain, I too have heard people on their death beds speak of wasted time, sometimes wasted lives, as they reviewed their lives, knowing death was just around the corner. We should not come to old age (if we are even granted old age) or our death beds with such regret of wasting the one life we were given.

The American journalist Hunter S. Thompson, though having lived a very turbulent and difficult life, once wrote, "Life should not be a journey to the grave with the intention of arriving safely in a pretty and well preserved body, but rather to skid in broadside in a cloud of smoke, thoroughly used up, totally worn out, and loudly proclaiming "Wow! What a Ride!" As Christians, the ride of our lives should be the peaceful and wonderful adventure of following Jesus Christ. Next time you take a trip, perhaps to the beach and pick up beautiful shells, enjoy the moment, thank God for the beauty of His creation, but ask Him how you can lead a meaningful, purposeful life lived for Him, and to be able to say to Him, "Wow! What a Ride!"

All In

What portion of our lives goes to Jesus? Do we give Jesus 100% or 99%, or maybe even 50% of our lives? Most of us would like to think we give 100%, but let's think about this concept for a moment. When I was a teenager in youth group, I remember hearing our youth pastor ask us if everything we did, everywhere we went, everything we looked at and listened to – if Jesus was sitting next to us, would we be embarrassed? Is every part of our life given to Jesus – 100%? Do we hold back on certain areas of our life that we want to keep for our own, where Jesus cannot participate? In John's letter as recorded in Revelation 21, he wrote that the Church (Christians), are the Bride of Christ. Compare our commitment to Jesus with a marriage: what if you told your spouse you would give him or her 99% of yourself in faithfulness, 364 days a year, but once a year you would give yourself to someone else? How would that work out?! Jesus does not want some of us, not even 99% of us, but He demands ALL of us, 365 days a year, in ever part of our lives – no exceptions.

In the Gospel of Mark, chapter 10, starting at verse 17, Jesus spoke to a rich young man who asked Him, "*What must I do to inherit eternal life?*" Jesus' response was, "*Go, sell your possessions and give the funds to the poor, and you shall have treasure in heaven: and come back and follow Me*" (Mark 10:21). Does this mean that everyone has to give away all of their money, or that we can earn our way to Heaven by our sacrifices and good works? No. The point Jesus was making is that in order to follow Him, we must give up everything for His sake. Jesus must come first and foremost in our lives, no matter the consequences. In the Sermon on the Mount, Jesus said, "*Seek first the kingdom of God and His righteousness, and all these things will be given to you as well"* (Matthew 6:33), meaning our life's needs and provisions. What did Jesus say is the most important commandment? In the Gospels, when speaking to His followers, Jesus quoted Deuteronomy 6:5, known as the Shema and said we must *"Love the Lord your God with all your heart and with all your soul and with all your strength."* Jesus said ALL- not some, not a portion, not even 99%, but ALL.

In the Gospels Jesus also told His followers that we must put Him first and foremost in life, above everyone and everything else. Jesus said, *"Whoever loves father or mother more than Me is not worthy of Me; and whoever loves son or daughter more than Me is not worthy of Me; and whoever does not take up his cross and follow Me is not worthy of Me. Those who find their life will lose it, and those who lose their life for My sake will find it"* (Matthew 10:37-39). Is there anyone or anything you love more than Christ or place before His commands?

We all should consider our lives, each and every part of them, and see if there is anything we are holding back on and any place we are not letting Jesus into, and make sure as the Bride of Christ, we are giving our all, 100%, 365 days a year. Through our prayers, our faith, and with the help of the Holy Spirit, let us ask God to enable us to do this – to be all in – ALL IN.

ℋ𝓪𝓻𝓶𝓸𝓷𝔂

No one needs to inform anyone that there is not very much harmony in our country and in our world. We have so many people protesting just about anything and everything; this side is against that side, this group refusing to even talk to or meet with that group, and there is far too much anger and discord. How apropos that here at the Lexington Rescue Mission we have recently been studying conflict resolution, which is a very important aspect of our Christian life. How should Christians deal with conflict and these types of problems? Scripture is very clear. 1 Peter 3:8 says, *"Finally, you must think the same thoughts, share difficulties with one another, having automatic interdependence with brotherly kindness; be tender-hearted and humble-minded."* Often times there is simply the matter of misunderstanding each other and not comprehending another person's position, which is where the discord begins, and a refusal to even listen. It seems like every day that I listen to the news there is more and more anger, shouting, rage, uncertainty, confusion, and hatred, even amongst those who call themselves Christians. Paul wrote to the Ephesian Christians, *"Let no unwholesome words come from your mouths, but only good words for enriching, that it may serve as a blessing to the hearers... Let your bitter frame of mind, anger and violent outbreak or brawling, and abusive language, be put away from you with all hatred; become gracious to one another, tenderly affectionate, ready to forgive one another, even as God for Christ's sake forgave you."* (Ephesians 4:29, 31& 32).

Why are we not adhering to the mandates of Scripture? Paul also wrote in his letter to the Colossians, *"As the consecrated, loved and select ones of God, clothe holy and dearly loved, clothe yourselves with a tender heart, kindness, humility, gentleness and long-suffering; be generous with each other and overlook faults, forgiving all disagreements as Christ forgave you. In addition to all these put on compassionate love, which binds believers together in perfect harmony"* (Colossians 3:12-14). Of course on this side of Heaven we will have strong disagreements, we will not see eye to eye, and we may even be baffled at how others see things so differently than we see them. As Christ-followers, our response is to be vastly different from the world. We are to be calm, peaceful, loving, and forgiving. We are not to display shouting, malice and anger. We are not to attack others verbally (or otherwise). We can sometimes simply agree to disagree, and let things go. We are to shine the light of Christ in a darkened and sin-filled world. We are also called to pray for those in authority over us – not fight them every inch of the way. Hebrews 13:17 says, *"Obey those who have rule over you, and line yourselves up under their authority: for they watch over your souls, because they know they will have an account to give. Make it a grateful task for them: it is your loss if they find it a difficult task."*No matter what our viewpoints and opinions are, no matter how much we agree or disagree with those around us, let us always be salt and light to the world, shining the love of Jesus through all we do and say, and as the apostle Paul said, *"let our gentleness be known to everyone"* (Philippians 4:5).

Proverbs for Living

My mother-in-law told me that she has been reading the book of Proverbs, and has really been enjoying them. She said to me, "If people just read these, they would know how to live!" I agreed. Proverbs, as in the whole of Scripture, does indeed give us the guidelines and wisdom we need to live our lives in every area. 2 Timothy 3:16 says, "*All Scripture is inspired by God and is useful for teaching, for reproof, for correction, and for training in righteousness, so that everyone who belongs to God may be proficient, equipped for every good work.*" We can only be equipped and proficient for good works, and for life, if we know God's Holy Word – the Bible, which is readily available to us all, at least here in America. If we are unsure of a decision or path to take in life, the Bible has the answer.

Several times I have had counseling clients who thought they might have easy answers and solutions to their particular problems, but they were outside of the parameters of the Bible. All I could tell them was that we must follow Scripture, even if doing so appears to be a more difficult road. God will bless our obedience – maybe not immediately, but the easy road is not always the right road. Proverbs 14:12 says, "*There is a way that seems right to a person, but its end is the way of death.*"

Prior to my working as a chaplain, I worked construction for many years as a painter. I worked in some very large high rise buildings in Chicago, as well as O'Hare airport. Without blueprints, we would have had no idea what to paint, what colors to use, and would be lost without the construction workers "bible" – the blueprints. Even if we were just painting a house, we still needed the blueprints to know what rooms to paint and what colors and finishes to use. Our Bible is our blueprint for life, in the large areas of our lives, as well as in the small or every day areas of life. We need to read God's Word each day in order to know what to do, how to live, what God expects of us, etc. The Bible is more than just a blueprint for life; it shows us who God is – His very nature, just how much He loves us, and the beautiful words of Scripture cause us to fall in love with Jesus.

As Christians, how in the world would we know what we are staking our lives and our eternity on, if we do not know who God is, what His Word says, and what He expects from us? Just as construction workers cannot wander around a building wondering what to build, or what types of paint to use and what colors go where without blueprints, the Architect of our lives has also laid out plans for us. We cannot just wander around through life guessing! Colossians 3:16 says, "*Allow the word of Christ to remain in you as a treasure of wisdom; teaching and gently reminding one another in psalms and hymns and spiritual songs...*" The Word of Christ, the Bible, will indeed give us wisdom... not just the book of Proverbs, but the entire Bible. This week, make it a priority to read the blueprints for your life, written by the greatest Architect ever. Let His perfect plan build a beautiful child of God.

Sacrifice

What do you think of when you hear the word, "sacrifice?" It usually has a negative connotation, such as being deprived, having to give up something we want or think we need - right? Who delights in sacrifice? One of the greatest theologians of all time, Saint Augustine, wrote a huge book called, *The City of God*, which all seminarians and theology students have to read, at least in part. In this great and massive book, Augustine made an interesting comment concerning sacrifice; he wrote that what is important is not what we sacrifice for God, or what we think we need to give up, but that we actually become the sacrifice for God. What does Augustine mean? We know that Jesus became our sacrifice for sin, so how do we become a sacrifice? The Apostle Paul wrote in his letter to the Roman Christians, "*I implore you, brethren, by the compassions of God that you place yourselves as a living sacrifice, consecrated and pleasing to God, which is your reasonable worship*" (Romans 12:1). Paul said we are to be a "*living sacrifice*," which is on-going and daily. We are the actual sacrifice, laying ourselves on God's altar as we die to self and live for Christ.

Paul wrote in his letter to the Ephesians, "*Become imitators of God, as His beloved children; and habitually behave in love, as Christ loved you, and was delivered for you as an offering and voluntary sacrifice to God to become a pleasing fragrance*" (Ephesians 5:1-2). As Jesus gave Himself fully over to His Father on our behalf, in love, we are also to give ourselves fully over to God as well.

We all make sacrifices at times for various reasons. Parents sacrifice a great deal for their children out of love. Spouses sacrifice for one another also out of love. We may sacrifice some of our time for our friends or our church – maybe even our jobs, again out of love. However, the sacrifices we make for others are occasional. Many of us sacrifice things during the Lenten season that we may enjoy, but again, that sacrifice is only temporary. God does not want our occasional or temporary sacrifice for Him – He wants every day, every moment to be lived as a sacrifice for Him, a lying down of our lives in submission to His will – even when we do not always understand what He is doing. Our sacrifice is also done out of love for our Savior, and our sacrifice to God must be continuous. Our sacrifice is our obedience to His will, to His call on our lives, and lays aside our own will in order to follow Him fully and completely. WE, our lives, are the sacrifice we offer to God. When we look towards the Cross, may we find joy and grace in the ultimate sacrifice Christ made for us, and in love, lay our lives and our will down for Him.

The Blessing of Relationships

One of the most wonderful, but also the most difficult and challenging things in life is our relationships. When we are in love and have good, healthy relationships, the world is a beautiful place. But when we are struggling with unhealthy, toxic, and even hateful relationships, the world can be a cold place indeed. In the Sermon on the Mount, Jesus spoke some very hard words concerning our relationships. He said, *"Whoever is angry with his brother without a cause shall be condemned by the court of justice: and whoever shall say to his brother, raca (I spit on you), shall be answerable to the Sanhedrin… Therefore if you bring your gift to the altar, and remember that your brother has a grievance against you; leave your gift before the altar, and first make peace with your brother and then return and offer your gift"* (Matthew 5:22-24). Jesus thought making peace and having good relationships was VERY important, and did not even want a gift brought to Him on the altar until peace was made between people.

Why are even the best relationships sometimes difficult? Because we are all sinful and imperfect people. Ever since the Fall back in the Garden of Eden, relationships have become challenging. When Adam and Eve sinned and God confronted them, Adam first blamed God by saying, *"The woman whom YOU gave to be with me"* (Genesis 3:12), as if he would have been just fine without her, even though God said, *"It is not good for man to be alone"* (Genesis 2:18). Then Adam blamed Eve, and there was discord between this first couple. When they had two sons, Cain and Abel, Cain became jealous and killed his brother; and ever since the very first humans sinned, relationships have been difficult.

As Christians, people are watching us and how we relate to others in our lives. At our various places of employment, what would our co-workers think if they heard us yelling at one another? What would our neighbors think if they consistently saw and heard us fighting and disrespecting our families? We must all learn to deal with our pride and our anger, which is often the root cause in relational conflicts. Proverbs 19:11 says, *"Good sense makes one slow to anger, and it is his glory to overlook an offense."*

Not only do we have Scripture to learn from in dealing with our relationships, but we also have the very nature and example of God to try and model, which we can indeed find in Scripture. Many times in the Bible it says that God is slow to anger. Are we? God is called compassionate, long suffering and forgiving. Are we? God is very kind and patient with us; are we with others? While we cannot love as God loves, we can try to model His love as much as we can through the power of the Holy Spirit who can empower us.

There is a wonderful book about resolving conflicts and building healthy relationships written by Ken Sande entitled *Peacemakers,* which I highly recommend. Jesus Himself said, *"Blessed are the peacemakers, for they shall be called sons of God"* (Matthew 5:9). We are called to peace and to love by our Heavenly Father, for all of the world to see. We need relationships in this world, and they should be a blessing to us. None of us can meet the challenges of life alone, but we need sisters and brothers in Christ, friends, and family, to walk with us through this often difficult life. Our relationships are God's gifts to us, and should not merely survive, but they should thrive.

Rising from the Dead

Some Christians in the ancient world called the raising of Lazarus "The Little Easter," as a foreshadowing of the real Easter to come, when Jesus Himself rose from the dead. Lazarus was a good friend of Jesus, and when he died, Jesus was grieved. *"Jesus wept"* (John 11:35) at His friends' grave; but, as we know, Jesus raised Lazarus from the dead. Jesus laid His life down for us. He broke the power of sin and death when He rose from the grave. Since Jesus did indeed rise from the dead, and gave us new life, He expects us to do something with it! The question is, "What will you do?"

I cannot imagine that Lazarus was not profoundly changed after he came back to life and even deeper in love with his friend Jesus after He called him forth from the grave. Those of us who are Christ- followers have symbolically been raised from the dead (which is signified in our baptisms), and also given new life, just as Lazarus, who, as we know, was physically raised from the dead. When we were saved, did our lives profoundly change? Are we deeper in love with Jesus more and more each day?

If we truly have accepted Christ into our lives to be our Lord and Savior, we are not only saved from the powers of sin and from eternal separation from God, but we have also been called to live radically new and different lives. God is the architect and builder of our lives, and, *"For our salvation is His handiwork, fashioned in Christ Jesus for good deeds, which God beforehand designed that good works should mark our behavior"* (Ephesians 2:10). Are we living according to God's Master plan for us, as drawn in His blueprints for each of our lives? Are we allowing God to work on us each day, building and forming us into His beautiful creation, as our Master Builder?

Those of us who follow Jesus are spiritually like Lazarus – we have been raised from the dead and given new life in Christ. Ephesians 2:1-2 says, "*And you He made alive, who were in disobedience and sins; for in the past you followed the ways of the world and lived in sin, and obeyed the prince of the air, the spirit that now works among the disobedient among whom we all once lived...*" We truly have been raised from the dead – from those things that caused death to our souls and eternal separation from God. Can you imagine the joy and amazement and excitement that must have been prevalent when Lazarus came out of his tomb? Did we have that same joy and amazement when we came out of our tombs of sin and from the power of death, and were brought to life through the power of the Holy Spirit? Are the people around us amazed at our transformation? Do others even see new life in us?

According to John chapter 12, many people came to see Jesus – the miracle worker who raised a man from the dead, and also to see Lazarus; what does a man look like who was dead, but now alive again? In the same manner, do people flock to us, to see what spiritually dead people who have been given new life in Christ look like? Do we look any different than before we accepted the love and salvation of Jesus Christ? We have been spiritually raised from the dead as new creatures in Christ. Like Lazarus, let us cause people to want to see who we are and what we "look like" as people born again through God's Holy Spirit.

The Starfish

Based on the story by Loren Eisley

"I awoke early, as I often did, just before sunrise to walk by the ocean's edge and greet the new day. As I moved through the misty dawn, I focused on a faint, far away motion. I saw a youth, bending and reaching and flailing his arms, dancing on the beach, no doubt in celebration of the perfect day soon to begin.

As I approached, I sadly realized that the youth was not dancing to the bay, but rather bending to sift through the debris left by the night's tide, stopping now and then to pick up a starfish and then standing, to heave it back into the sea. I asked the youth the purpose of the effort. "The tide has washed the starfish onto the beach and they cannot return to the sea by themselves," the youth replied. "When the sun rises, they will die, unless I throw them back to the sea."

As the youth explained, I surveyed the vast expanse of beach, stretching in both directions beyond my sight. Starfish littered the shore in numbers beyond calculation. The hopelessness of the youth's plan became clear to me and I countered, "But there are more starfish on this beach than you can ever save before the sun is up. Surely you cannot expect to make a difference."

The youth paused briefly to consider my words, bent to pick up a starfish and threw it as far as possible. Turning to me he simply said, 'I made a difference to that one.'

I left the boy and went home, deep in thought of what the boy had said. I returned to the beach and spent the rest of the day helping the boy throw starfish in to the sea."

The needs in this world are great. We look around at the world's problems and needs and they seem overwhelming; we know that we simply cannot help everyone with everything they need. There is an African Proverb that says, "If you think you are too small to make a difference, try sleeping in a closed room with a mosquito." In Africa, malaria is carried by mosquitos, and if a person is bitten by a carrying mosquito, that very tiny insect can make someone very, very sick. In other words, even the smallest of creatures can indeed make a huge difference in a person's life. Having traveled to several countries in Africa over the past 18 years, I completely understand how much difference a tiny mosquito can make!

Occasionally at the mission, we are asked to tell about a client whose life was changed. I must admit, that is often difficult. Many of our clients do not change or do not have any real desire to change; however, once in a while there is indeed a story of someone who heard the Gospel, felt the love of Jesus here, and truly had a desire to change their life. Like the one starfish which was thrown back into the water, that one life here at the Mission matters. Jesus said that if we merely give food to the hungry, drinks to the thirsty, clothing to the naked, a welcoming place to the stranger, if we care for the sick and visit the prisoner, and do these things to "the least of these," we are showing acts of love not only in His name, but also to Him (Matthew 25:31-46). God will take care of the results; we simply do our part as He commanded. Many pastors, missionaries, chaplains (and anyone who works full time in ministry), often get burnt out because there are not as many "success" stories as they would like. In my work at the Mission, I sometimes feel that same burnout. If and when we do feel discouraged, remember the starfish. It's simply one life at a time, and we can all make a difference for that one.

Where there's Smoke....

I love doing yard work. When the weather begins to warm up, I enjoy getting the yard ready, turning the flower and vegetable gardens over to prepare for planting, clear out the old, dead brush and leaves under the bushes, and get ready for Spring. We have a small un-used farm behind our house and the brush grew all over our fence, so I decided to clear it out. For hours I cleared away brush and began to burn it in our small portable fire pit. I also enjoy the smell of burning leaves and I enjoy watching the fire, reminiscent of my camping days as a child, and something I still very much enjoy. The other day I wanted to pile up more brush to burn, so I dumped the massive heap of yesterday's ash out back near the farm so I could pile up more brush to burn. As I was finishing up my work, I looked at the time and knew I had to get in the shower and start getting ready for work. My feet got tangled up in some vines, which I began to cut away, and which prevented me from getting to the house as planned. As I began to untangle myself, I smelled the pleasant aroma of burning leaves, and wondered who else was out working in their yard. To my horror, it was me! The ashes I had dumped were still hot from the day before, and I saw smoke rising near the brush that was next to the trees and my house! In a panic, I got a metal rake and began beating the ground, and then ran in the house for pitchers of water. My hose was rolled up in the garage, the outside water turned off from the winter with straw around the water source. I ran into the garage, grabbed the hose, threw off the straw, hooked up the hose and turned on the water to put out the smoldering leaves; I knew of course that where there is smoke, there will soon be fire!

After I completely flooded the area where I had dumped the ash, I went into the house and thought about how God protects us – often in ways we know, such as in this debacle; but also I am sure many times of which we are not even aware. God protected me by the annoyance of getting my feet tangled up to stop me from going into the house. Maybe some of our annoyances are really God at work, protecting us from some unseen danger. I may try to keep that in mind from now on! Scripture says, "*The Lord protects him and keeps him…*" (Psalm 41:2). The Psalms are filled with the protection and deliverance of God. Another beautiful Psalm is 91:14-15, says, "*Those who love Me, I will deliver; I will protect those who know My name. When they call to Me, I will answer them; I will be with them in trouble, I will rescue them and honor them.*" 1 John 5:18 speaks of God protecting us from our enemy as well – Satan: "*The one born of God keeps clear of sin; because his divine origin protects him, and the evil one cannot lay a hand on him.*" God protects us not only from physical danger, but also from spiritual danger. Jesus also prayed for His followers shortly before His own death. In Jesus' beautiful prayer to His Father, He said, "*I am no more in the world, but these are in the world, and I am coming to You. Holy Father, keep though Your own authority those You gave Me, so that they may be one, as we are one*" (John17:11).

God truly does protect us in so many ways - physically and spiritually, and again, in so many ways that we may not even know. This week, let us try to be mindful of annoyances, remembering that they may possibly be God working through them for our good. Let us also be thankful for the protections God does indeed give us, and be thankful for Jesus' love in asking His Father to watch over us while we are in this world.

Smoldering Leaves

In my previous devotion, I wrote about how I almost set my house and surrounding neighborhood on fire… thank God for His protection! There is another lesson in my blunder. I thought about the smoldering leaves, just waiting to ignite in fire after I unknowingly threw hot ashes onto the pile. The water I sprayed onto them and the pounding of the metal rake fortunately put the fire out before the flames caught, while the leaves were still just smoldering. The smoldering leaves smelled good, reminding me of the "fleeting pleasures of sin" (Hebrews 11:25). Sin, like burning leaves, if left to smolder, will also create a disaster!

In the Sermon on the Mount, Jesus taught some very difficult lessons. Among them, He said that if we so much as hate our brother (or sister), we commit murder in our hearts. If we just look upon a person with lust, and never even touch that person, it is as if we commit adultery, since Jesus said we commit adultery in our hearts (Matthew 5:21-22 & 27-28). If we allow anger, lust, or any other negative, non-productive emotion to smolder within us, eventually it will indeed ignite into a fire that will burn and hurt us and others, and can get out of control. Proverbs 6:27-28 says, *"Can a man scoop fire into his lap without his clothes being burned? Can a man walk on hot coals without his feet being scorched?"* If we allow our thoughts to wander too far and too dark, eventually those smoldering thoughts might be acted upon and ignite into a fire we cannot extinguish or control.

Jesus knows the human mind – He created it. Sin, all sin, begins in our minds and hearts, which needs to be protected under the love and grace of God. One of the saddest verses in the Bible, in my opinion, is John 2:24-25, which says, *"But Jesus did not commit Himself to them, because He knew the nature of men, and needed no additional witness of man: for He knew the nature of man."* Jesus knows we are sinful and in dire need of His Holy Spirit to live within us and to give us His abundant grace and mercy when we fall. As sinful human beings, we will indeed fall, and God forgives us, but as Jesus told the Samaritan woman at the well, *"Go and sin no more"* (John 8:11). While we are still sinners who will never be perfect on this side of Heaven, we can indeed live in the power of the Holy Spirit where He can prevent our smoldering sins from igniting and getting out of control. With God's love, He can quench the danger that sin always brings and strengthen us when we are tempted. While I do love the smell of burning leaves, they can be dangerous if left unattended and will surely ignite if not put out. This week, and always, we need to be aware of any smoldering sins and make sure we quench them through the power of the Holy Spirit who is always ready to keep us in His perfect peace and safety.

The Phoenix

Lately at work, we have attempted to try to start spiritual conversations during lunch with our clients, so I wrote a couple of questions on the blackboard in the lunch room: What does Easter mean to you and what is your favorite Easter memory? I received a couple of good answers, some not so well-thought-out answers, and one answer which I have heard before: one man asked if I knew about the pagan origins of Easter. I replied I had; however, I mentioned that Christians celebrate the risen Christ on Easter, even though we may not be certain of the exact date, regardless of pagan stories and myths. Easter is the greatest and most joyful Christian celebration of the year.

Pagan origins reminded me of a very old myth of which my painting company that I used to own was named after: The Phoenix. Perhaps some of you are familiar with this story. The Phoenix was a beautiful, legendary bird that lived in Arabia, and, according to this pagan myth, consumed itself by fire every 500 years. A new, young Phoenix which was just as colorful and breathtaking then sprang from its ashes. Upon its impending death, it builds a nest, sets itself on fire, and is consumed by the flames, and then the new Phoenix springs forth from the pyre. Only one Phoenix can exist at a time.

Early Christian tradition adopted the Phoenix as a symbol of both immortality and resurrection, and the magnificent creature is seen as a symbol of renewal, rebirth, and starting anew. In John 3:16, Jesus told Nicodemus that he (and all of us), must be "*born again*" to receive new life in Him. Our old lives and sinful nature do indeed need to be burned up, to allow God to make us into a new creation – stunning creatures who are the "*light of the world*" (Matthew 5:14).

The myth of the Phoenix, according to classical and early Christian traditions, also speaks of the palms that are used on Palm Sunday, which are evergreen, and are a symbol of perpetual renewal that correlates with the imagery associated with the dying and reborn Phoenix. In the fourth and fifth centuries, Church Fathers (including Ambrose, Cyril of Jerusalem, and Jerome), were still repeating the myth, and some began offering it as a God-given proof of the reality of Christ's resurrection. In the words of Cyril, "God knew men's unbelief and provided for this purpose a bird, called a Phoenix" (Catechetical Lecture 18).

Around the sixth century, an anonymous Coptic preacher wrote a sermon in which he compared the legendary bird to the Truth of the resurrection. Little by little, Christian writers began to read more into the various references to the strange creature. They noted its uniqueness ("the only one of its kind") and began to interpret the Phoenix of pagan myth not only as a Christian symbol of virgin birth, renovation and resurrection, but also as an allegory of Jesus Christ Himself.

At various times I have heard people criticize some Christian holidays as stemming from pagan beliefs or rituals. The truth of the resurrection and the Holy Spirit who gives us new life when we are born again, can reach all people in all cultures, when we contextualize the Gospel through stories or myths that others are familiar with; after all, is that not the work of missionaries? The apostle Paul said he "*can become all things to all people, that I might by all means save some*" (1 Corinthians 9:22). Paul spoke to various different philosophers such as the Stoics, about their own philosophies, and then contextualized them to show them the Truth of the Gospel of Jesus Christ; we can do that too. As we share the true story of the Cross and the

Resurrection, let us be sensitive to other people's beliefs, take time to understand them, and then through whatever means the Holy Spirit gives us, share the wonderful Truth of Jesus Christ and Him risen.

Nothing but the Best

Almost daily, we experience inconveniences, and from time to time we go through major difficulties in life, but God works through all of our circumstances to build our faith, strengthen our character, test our obedience, and make us ready for His Kingdom. As Christians, we know that our Lord is always near, walking each step with us, though more often than not, He is carrying us. We are never on our own.

The Apostle Paul knew of great hardships during his ministry. He wrote in 2 Corinthians 4:8-11, "*We are pressed on every side, yet not hemmed in, we are bewildered, but never at a loss; persecuted, but not abandoned; knocked down, but never counted out; always exposed to the dying body, but remembering the death of the Lord Jesus, that the life of Jesus might be revealed in our body. For though we live we are perpetually delivered unto death for Jesus' sake, that the life of Jesus may be made operative in our mortal body.*" The good that can come from our suffering and difficulties is that we have the privilege of showing who Jesus is as He lives and works through us. We are always to show who Jesus is to the world.

Some of our problems in life are indeed big, and others are simply minor annoyances; but, either way, we must remember to reflect Jesus – something that is not always easy! One minor example of an inconvenience was here at the Mission: some of us experienced moves from our offices that perhaps were rather inconvenient and took us out of our comfort zones, but were really not a big deal at all. I found a corner of the building to place my desk, computer, Bible, paperwork, etc., which I need, and our Executive Director laughingly said about my new work area that it was, "nothing but the best." I said I was thrilled that I even found a place to work, but I surely did not consider it "the best," even though it is only a minor, temporary inconvenience.

When we complain about minor step backs or inconveniences in life (which we all do), we need to remember that when we are living in God's will, He may place circumstances before us that may not appear to be "the best," but they are for our own good and for God's purposes. Romans 8:28 says, "*We know that all things work together for good for those who love God, who are called according to His purpose.*" God is always working through life's circumstances, inconveniences, and difficulties for our good, to mold us into the type of people He desires, and to reflect His character.

All that God does for us or allows in our lives is truly for our best, even though it may appear differently. Jesus endured the Cross (something we will never even come close to understanding), which was a horrible punishment of torture; but He lovingly and willingly endured that awful death so that indeed we can experience, "nothing but the best," both here on earth and for eternity! That Cross surely did not appear to be a good thing, but Jesus remained humble unto death, and even forgave those who were killing Him. Who among us could do that?! When we go through trials, difficulties and inconveniences as followers of Christ, let us pause and remember that our Heavenly Father always has in mind for us, "nothing but the best!"

Thinking of Others

Most parents and grandparents brag about their kids and grandkids; there is nothing wrong with that. We should be proud of our family and make sure our children and grandchildren know that we are indeed proud of them. We should be proud though not only of their accomplishments, but more so for their character – for who are kids and grandkids are as human beings. Let me share a story:

My son Joshua is a high school English teacher. He has worked very hard both in his education and as a teacher. He has a Master's Degree that he earned on a full academic scholarship. Last year he was awarded Teacher of the Year for his entire County. He works at an alternative school with very troubled students – most who, unfortunately, will end up in prison or an early grave. On an almost daily basis, he deals with physical altercations from his students, and always hears vile language and threats as he simply tries to teach English. Most of the students do not listen or pay attention as he lectures to the top of heads, face down on desks. Most students are under the influence of drugs and/or alcohol. After years of working in this frustrating environment, my son applied at several other high schools in order to find employment elsewhere. He called me to tell me of an interview he recently had that went very well, with a great chance of obtaining new work, but for which he said, "He could not accept."

My son is a tenured teacher, and a good teacher. He currently has a job and is guaranteed his position next year. He interviewed alongside a non-tenured teacher, for this teacher's current position. The principle and others on the interview team, for some reason, interviewed both my son and this other non-tenured English teacher together, at the exact same time, side by side! While none of us understood this method, my son saw that this teacher was nervous, knowing he was interviewing simply to keep his job, alongside last year's tenured Teacher of The Year. Both my son and this other teacher have wives and daughters, and both need their jobs. When Joshua completed the interview, he went home and said he could not sleep that night; he felt sadness for the man he competed with for a job. That night, Joshua emailed the principle of the school where he interviewed, as well as the other teacher he interviewed with and of whom he competed. Joshua thanked them for the chance to interview for the position, and said he could not even consider taking this job if it were offered. Why would he not jump at the chance for a teaching position at another school? Because of his faith and the Word of God.

Joshua said he was reminded of the story in 2 Samuel 12 of King David, after he had committed adultery with Bathsheba and had her husband Uriah killed in battle. The prophet Nathan boldly confronted King David and told him a story about a poor old man who had only one little lamb, and how a rich man with many sheep came and took this man's lamb, which he loved so much, and prepared it for his dinner guest, leaving the poor man with nothing. King David was enraged at this story, but Nathan told David that HE was that man – having taken a man's only wife of whom he loved, when rich king David already had wives and an entire kingdom!

The following morning, Joshua received an email from this fellow teacher, who said he was responding with tears in his eyes at the love and mercy of his Creator, who he believes has been testing his faith in the matter of his job, and was so grateful for Joshua's attitude. This man proceeded to say that not only does he have a little daughter, but that his wife has had four miscarriages, and is currently thirteen weeks pregnant, so he has not told her that he has to interview to try to keep his job for fear that the stress may cause her to lose yet another baby. This other teacher said he believes in a good God who is faithful, loving, and just, and was so grateful to see a Christian man live out his faith, regardless of the consequences.

Living out the holy Word of God is indeed a call to a selfless life, of which we can only do through the power of the Holy Spirit. Galatians 2:19 says that we, *"have been crucified with Christ, and it is no longer I who live, but Christ who lives in me."* As Christ followers, we can no longer live for ourselves, but only as Christ calls us to live – for Him and for the good of others. Thank you for allowing me to take this week to share a story about my son, who looks to his Heavenly Father for guidance in this life, no matter what the circumstances. I am reminded that we need to always look to our glorious God, who alone can enable us to even begin to want to live a selfless life.

My World

One beautiful summer day I was driving my four year old granddaughter home from the park, when she looked out of the car window and said, "Where are we? We look like we're back in my world." She lives in a very nice sub-division, of mostly two-story brick homes. I live in a small house outside of town, across from a small horse farm, with just a few other small homes around me. We were driving past nice two-story brick homes as we were leaving the park, so I knew what she meant about "her world." My granddaughter's comment struck me as both funny and profound.

As Christians, we should live in a world that looks very different from the secular world, and our world should be obviously different to others. Jesus said in Matthew 5, "*You are the light of the world. A city on a hill cannot be hidden. Neither do people light a lamp and put it under a bowl. Instead they put it on a stand, and it gives light to everyone in the house. In the same way, let your light shine before men, that they may see your good works and glorify your Father in heaven*" (Matthew 5:14-16). In Jesus' Sermon on the Mount, which is recorded in Matthew chapters 5, 6 & 7 , He gave descriptions of how His followers are to live (which are radically different from how the rest of the world lives), such as loving our enemies, not worrying about money or accumulating material wealth, and rejoicing in persecutions. The world Jesus calls us to live in, for His glory, is a world that perhaps others may not understand, and which looks radically different from their own world. Jesus also said that we, "*If you were of the world, the world would naturally haves affection for you; but because you are not of the world, because I selected you out of this world."* Jesus went on to say, *"Therefore the world hates you"* (John 15:19).

Is our world any different from the world of unbelievers? Like a four year old child, can we and others recognize it as being different? Do we live in a world where we freely forgive others who have done us great harm, and then pray for them? Do we live in a world where we care more about the needs of the poor than ourselves? Do we live in a world where we give not out of our surplus, but sacrificially? Do we live in a world where we ask God to use us wherever, however, and whenever He chooses, rather than making our own plans and running them by God for His approval? Do we live in a world where our tongues are bridled and we do not speak hurtful words or seek revenge for wrongs committed against us? Do we live in a world where we do not always have to be right, where we pursue the good of others, and where we think more of other people than ourselves? Jesus calls us to live in such a world that is not possible on our own, but can be lived through the power of the Holy Spirit. This week, and always, let's pray for God to move us into another world other than our own, and pursue love, all for His glory, that all the world may see.

Summer Days

There is something about summer that slows most of us down. One reason is simply the temperatures. When it is hot outside, many people find it a little more difficult to move as quickly as when it is cold. Kids are out of school and sleep later than usual, many people's schedules have changed, teachers are off from work, and some families take vacations. Summer is often a season to slow down. Despite the fact that I do not like hot weather, I do like summer for many reasons: flowers are in bloom, grass is green, trees are full, and there is an abundance of outdoor activities I enjoy. Like most people, I slow down (a bit).

For many, many years, my schedule was so hectic, that I used to say I did not have time to think or to feel. My life zipped past me and I felt like I was on auto pilot. Now that I am older, my life has drastically changed for the better, and I can contemplate, reflect, and consider. The book of Ecclesiastes says, "*In the day of prosperity be joyful, and in the day of adversity, consider*" (Ecclesiastes 7:14). In order to consider, we must stop our constant business. To consider, we must think, reflect, learn, and like nature, grow. Why "consider" in the day of adversity? Consider what? I had a good pastor friend who used to tell me that when we are in, "*the day of adversity*," there is always something to learn. We need to press into God, into His Word, quiet ourselves before the Lord, and listen to His voice. We need to consider what God is trying to tell us or teach us through our adversities. We must also remember that he is right there with us, and will carry us when needed. We are never alone in our troubles.

We all go through various seasons of life. There are times when we are on the run with hectic schedules, and other times when we are able to slow down a bit. Sometimes we are in a season of joy, but other times, we are in seasons of loss and sadness. Romans 12:15 says, "*Share the happiness of those who rejoice, and share the sorrow of those who are sad.*" As Christians, we need to be in tune with the various seasons that not only we, but that others are also going through, and indeed share their joys and their sorrows. We can only share these seasons with our brothers and sisters when we can slow down enough to pay attention, which can sometimes be challenging. I Corinthians 12: 26 explains how Christians are all part of one Body – the Body of Christ, and says, "*If one member suffers, all suffer together with it; if one member is honored, all rejoice together with it.*"

My prayer is that I am able to slow down enough to share in the seasons of life with others, especially those in the Body of Christ. Perhaps this summer, this very warm season in life, we can take more time to read God's Word, become more attuned to the feelings and circumstances of others, such as those in our families, in our churches, in our communities and in our workplaces, and share with others all that God brings our way. God desires us to be in community, and reminds us that, "*For everything there is a season, and a time for every matter under heaven*" (Ecclesiastes 3:1). May we bask in the warmth of God's love this summer season, and reflect, consider, and contemplate all God is doing in our lives.

Meaning in Life

Sadly but true, it seems that on an almost daily basis we hear about terrorism in some part of the world. I often wonder how so many people can be so misguided, and what "radicalizes" some people to the point of cold-blooded murder of innocent people of whom they do not even know. I have been reading much about this topic and listening to many commentators, in search of some reasons. In the UK, there have been three major attacks in the past three months. Why? One commentator stated bluntly, that the radical terrorists approach young people who have no real direction, goal, or purpose in life, and ask them if they want to waste their lives "eating fish and chips and watching football, or if they want to have real meaning and purpose in life, as well as securing a place in Paradise for eternity." Terrorism is their answer to this question.

Most people would say they want their lives to amount to something meaningful and to feel they have some purpose on this earth. All people who believe in an afterlife want to go to Paradise. I wonder though: how many of us Christians are approaching others and asking these same questions as the terrorists ask, but can instead point people to the Truth of Jesus Christ, who came to love, serve and forgive, and who calls us to do the same? Through loving God and others as ourselves, and by trusting in the redeeming work of Christ on the Cross, we truly can secure our place in Paradise – a Heavenly home where we will forever worship our God and Creator, and be in loving community with all believers from all times, face to face with Jesus.

Jesus told His disciples (as well as us today), "*Do not let your life be troubled: you believe in God; believe also in Me. There are many dwelling- places in my Father's House: if it were not so, I would have told you. I am going there to prepare a place for you"* (John 14:1&2). We can know with certainty that we have a place in Paradise, not because of anything we do, but because we trust in the power of Jesus who broke the curse of sin and death. No warped sense of a "heroic" act of our own delusions will save us. The only truly heroic act that saves is the sacrificial death and crucifixion of Jesus Christ, who took on the sins of the world, and then most of all, His resurrection from the dead.

Satan came to *"kill, steal and destroy"* (John 10:10a) and one of the ways he is accomplishing that is through terrorism. Satan is the, *"father of lies"* (John 8:44) and Jesus said *"your enemy the devil, prowls about as an angry, seeking someone to greedily consume"* (1 Peter 5:8). Satan is unfortunately devouring many people. Their end is death and eternal destruction, where they will be face to face with Satan. The apostle Paul wrote, *"For our wrestling is not against a physical enemy, but against evil princes of darkness who rule this world, against hosts of spiritual wickedness in heavenly warfare"* (Ephesians 6:12). In that same context, Paul said that we can *"put on the full armor of God so that you can take your stand against the devil's schemes"* (Ephesians 6:11). Our mighty God is stronger than Satan, and He is waiting to equip us with all we need to combat the lies of the enemy, which come to us every day in a variety of ways.

As Christ-followers, we need to share the beautiful and merciful love of our Savior with others, and point to a meaningful way of life that involves more than perhaps living for the weekend or watching football. Jesus said He came to give us an abundant life (John 10:10b), filled with meaning and purpose, which never involves hatred and killing, but is a life filled with love, joy, peace, forgiveness, serving, and even loving our enemies and praying for them to turn to Christ for that same meaning. We need not live in fear, but in prayer for our enemies, and to tell others about the meaning and purpose they can have in their lives by following Jesus Christ, who alone can save, and who alone can give us true life.

Living Out Our Call

I have a missionary friend who travels primarily to the Middle East to talk with Muslims, to try and open dialogue with them on religion, share Jesus with them, and frequently talks with Imam's, who are the leaders of the Muslim religion. He has recently returned from Iraq and Afghanistan in his work, and spoke about the terrorism that occurs there on a very frequent basis. While he was in Afghanistan, one German woman was shot in her home, two foreign workers were kidnapped and held hostage, and a suicide blast killed 90 people. He left when Americans were urged to leave the country because of deteriorating security and terrorist threats. He has a prayer team that prays for him daily, of which I am a part, and works through a mission organization that keeps close tabs on his whereabouts. I told my friend that I have great respect for him and did not think I could do what he does, being such dangerous work. He simply said, "We have each been built for a specific task. May God find us faithfully doing what each of us was made to do."

My missionary friend believes God called him to work with the Muslims, build relationships with them, and show them Jesus and the Truth of the Cross. He believes that if God has called him to work in the Middle East with Muslims, he must do that work, despite the danger. In 2009 I went to work in Calcutta, India for about a month, and sadly to say, I told God that if He called me to do mission work in Calcutta, I would probably pull a Jonah and head the other direction. I did not like Calcutta. I pray my faith and obedience has matured since then.

Satan can interfere with God's call on our lives through fears, unpleasant conditions and surroundings, or many other factors that keep us from living out God's Call on our lives. The word *sabotage* is a French word for a wooden shoe. Sabotage was the act of throwing a wooden shoe into machinery to stop work. The word sabotage now means any attempt to stop production or ruin a product. Satan tries to sabotage our work and prevent us from accomplishing God's plan and purpose for our lives. Is there anything Satan is doing in your life to sabotage God's plan for you? Fortunately, I never felt God calling me to India, but if He did, the wooden shoe Satan would have thrown into my life was the extreme poverty, noise, and ugliness of that city. Maybe your wooden shoe is an addiction or a bad habit. Maybe it is fear. Maybe that wooden shoe being thrown into your machine is an unwillingness to give up your comfortable life-style. We all have areas in our lives that Satan can, and does sabotage.

The apostle Paul often wrote in his letters that he was, *"called by the will of God to be a messenger of Jesus Christ"* (I Corinthians 1:1) and that he could not help but preach the Gospel (I Corinthians 9:16) since that is what God called him to do with his life. For those of us who work at the Mission, and feel this work is God's call for our lives, I came across an appropriate quote from Jimmy Fortune of the Statler Brothers (an old musical group) in "The Gideon" magazine of which I could relate. He said, *"This is what my life is about – planting little seeds of hope in places where the dirt might be a little hard and dry."* For most of us, our call may not be to travel as missionaries to the Middle East like my friend, but we can surely do what God calls us to do right here at the Lexington Rescue Mission, or wherever He calls us in the future. My prayer is that I never pull a Jonah, but will follow wherever God leads, and may He find me faithfully doing what I was made to do.

Making Plans

In the summer months, many people plan vacations; some of us will be making plans for a trip, or maybe just for some time away from work. I like to camp and not make too many plans for my trips other than the basic direction I will be heading, primarily because I have no idea what I will see along the way, what areas of the country I like and may wish to remain in, and what areas and campgrounds I may not particularly like or wish to stay in. While thinking about my upcoming vacation, I am reminded of the Proverb, *"The human mind plans the way, but the Lord directs the steps"* (Proverbs 16:9). I have also heard the saying (not from the Bible), "Man plans; God laughs." We all may approach plans differently, but ultimately, we must remember that God knows the past, the present, and the future, and while He never forces anyone to follow Him, He does indeed direct our paths.

I have made plans in the past that have failed miserably, sometimes causing me some disappointment, frustration, and yes, even anger; but it is often in retrospect that I see what God was doing, and was doing for my good. I am thankful that many of my own plans did not come to fruition, because I saw a much greater plan later on, for which I am most thankful. I am sure many of you have similar stories. Romans 8:28 says, *"We know that all things work together for good for those who love God, who are called according to His purpose."* God has plans for us all in our lives, and we should pray earnestly for Him to show us our purpose. No life is a mistake, and God placed us here to reflect His glory and bring others to Him and to the salvation He so generously offers.

Many of us have heard the scripture, *"For surely I know the plans I have for you, says the Lord, plans for your welfare and not for harm, to give you a future and a hope. Then when you call upon Me and come and pray to Me, I will hear you. When you search for Me, you will find Me; if you seek Me with all your heart, I will let you find me, says the Lord"* (Jeremiah 29:11). We may still make plans that fail, that were not God's will for us, even when they seemed so right, but we can rest in our faith that God is working behind the scenes to bring about His plans that are even better.

Here at the Mission we have seen plans that appeared beneficial and godly, yet they did not come to fruition, and it is so wonderful to see the faith of everyone stretch and grow as we trust God's will for us as His servants. In my opinion, the most beautiful portion of the Scripture in Jeremiah, is that God's best plan for us is that in our searching, He will let us find Him. He will not ignore any who desire Him, but will come to all who want Him. We do not serve a distant creator or an uninvolved god, but we have the opportunity to have a loving, intimate relationship with the God of the Universe, the God who created each one of us, and who even makes it possible to search and seek after Him. Our God has many wonderful plans for us to live out the abundant and satisfying life that only He can offer.

Whether we make plans in our lives or fly by the seat of our pants, we can rest in the fact that our Heavenly Father, our Lord and Savior, has beautiful plans for us and will not leave us alone, but will guide and direct our steps right into His merciful and loving arms.

Preparations

Life is filled with change, sometimes good or exciting, and sometimes perhaps not so good. One thing change does bring us though, are new challenges. Challenges and adventures can be either exciting or frightening, perhaps depending on our faith and whether or not we are prepared. Jesus calls us many times throughout Scripture to be prepared in this life for whatever comes our way. God even made preparations for the coming of Jesus to this earth through John the Baptist. In the gospel of Mark we read, *"According to the sacred writings of the prophet Isaiah, 'Watch, I send my herald before you, to prepare the way; the voice crying aloud in the desert, make His path without delay"* (Mark 1:2-3). John prepared the way in teaching the people about repentance for the forgiveness of sins, for which Jesus explicitly came. God also prepared things for us, which the apostle Paul wrote in his letter to the Ephesians: *"For our salvation in His handiwork, fashioned in Christ Jesus for good deeds, which God beforehand designed that good works should mark our behavior"* (Ephesians 2:10). Our way of life is to do good works, and we are to prepare ourselves during this life not only for living out God's call for lives, but also for the life to come.

This week I was told of an unexpected death of a regular lunch client who was only 50 years old, Jesse, who died, they say, "of natural causes," though he was relatively young. He did though, always carry around with him a large bag of medications and complained of frequent health problems. I wonder if he had ever prepared for his death? Do we? Do we prepare daily for the battles we will face in this life, such as loss, sin, and the unknown? How does the Bible teach us to prepare?

In Ephesians 6, we read of putting on the armor of God, "*so that you may be able to stand against the strategy and assault of the adversary*" (Ephesians 6:11). Paul wrote to the Ephesian Christians in chapter 6:10-17, that we can indeed stand strong in the Lord, prepared, and ready to face whatever comes our way by taking up the whole armor of God, and only then will be able to stand firm. Paul wrote that, "*Our struggle is not against enemies of blood and flesh, but against the rulers, against the authorities, against the cosmic powers of this present darkness, against the spiritual forces of evil in the heavenly places*" (Ephesians 6:12).

Peter also wrote about the spiritual preparations we must make when he wrote, "*Rid your minds of every encumbrance, keep full control of your senses, and set your hopes on the gift that is offered you when Jesus Christ appears*" (1 Peter 1:13). There are many things in life we need to prepare for: sending our children off to school at the end of summer, or our older children away to college, or maybe we are beginning an educational program. We might need to prepare for new jobs, moves to other states, marriage, and many other changes in life which require planning and preparations. While we prepare for these various events in our lives, we need to also make spiritual preparations every day. Perhaps as summer winds down and we begin a new season, we too can consider our spiritual preparations, and remember to put on the whole armor of God: the belt of truth, the breastplate of righteousness, shoes to proclaim the Gospel of peace, the shield of faith, the helmet of salvation, and the sword of the Spirit. As you get dressed each morning, think about adding some spiritual clothing as well, in order to be ready for whatever the day may bring.

Just Passing Through

If you have ever traveled to another country where the culture is very different, most likely you felt like an outsider, an alien, and a stranger: words and phrases were probably unfamiliar, or maybe you did not understand the language at all, and the customs, the manners, and the expectations were probably different from your "norm." Various cultures differ on what they consider "appropriate" dress, so perhaps you wore something that was perfectly acceptable in America, but totally unacceptable in another country. Food and eating/ socializing customs may have also been very different from what you are accustomed to; and, it is possible you might have offended someone without your knowledge. Time is perceived and adhered to vastly different from culture to culture as well. Perhaps people viewed you as strange since you did not live within their culture, but brought your own culture to theirs, and there was a clash. That same cultural clash exists amongst Christians who live in an un-Christian world: we clash with non-Christians as far as our world view and what we think is appropriate, or right and wrong.

We may often feel like the world does not make sense, people do not understand us, and our values are very different from what we see around us; it is because we truly are not of this world, but rather we are a, *"peculiar people"* (1 Peter 2:9 KJV) who have been called out of darkness into the light of Jesus Christ. There is an old Christian rock song written by Larry Norman who sang, "This world is not my home, I'm just passing through." Our real home is indeed in Heaven, not here on this earth, and this world and those who do not belong to Christ have a very different perspective and philosophy of life than do Christ followers. The "Hall of Faith" chapter in the Bible, Hebrews 11 says of the faithful men and women of God, *"All these died without possessing the promises. They only saw them from afar and greeted them from afar, and they admitted that they were strangers and sojourners upon the earth...they were reaching out for something better, a heavenly country"* (Hebrews 11:13 &16A).

Peter wrote in one of his letters, *"Peter, an apostle of Jesus Christ, to God's elect, strangers in the world..."* (I Peter 1:1) and again, *"Beloved, I urge you, as strangers and sojourners..."* (I Peter 2:11). We are indeed strangers here if we truly follow the teachings of Jesus, which do not conform to the teachings of those outside of the Kingdom. We are not to be conformed to this world, but as the letter to the Romans says, we are instead, *"to be conformed to the image of God's Son"* (Romans 8:29). Jesus said, *"Since the world hates you, know that it has hated Me before it hated you. If you were of the world, the world would naturally have affection for you: but because you are not of the world, because I have selected you out of the world, therefore the world hates you" (John 15:18).* Praise God we belong to Him, and His love covers us completely.

When you feel like an outsider, when you are not understood, when your viewpoints and opinions clash with the world, rejoice in the fact that your real home is not here on earth, but is in Heaven, where we will all be one in Christ Jesus. Paul wrote, *"At the present we see only blurred reflections in polished metal; but then face to face the blurred image will be gone and we will see ourselves as God sees us"* (I Corinthians 13:12). We will someday be complete with Jesus, who, with open arms, will finally welcome us home, and where clashes and misunderstandings will be no more.

The Excitement of a Child

My husband and I worked at the county fair last week with the Gideon's, passing out New Testaments; unfortunately, many people were not interested in taking one. For the six hours that we were there, we only handed out 104 Testaments. We were told this number was down from previous years, but we were happy for the 104 people who did receive God's Word. We were also told that some of the people who take the New Testaments do not keep them, but leave them lying somewhere on the fairgrounds. Some people even throw them in the trash; that was a bit discouraging. At the Gideon meeting a few days later, we learned of something very encouraging that happens each year with those scattered Testaments: the primary food vendor for the county fair picks them up, saves them, and uses them for the Samaritan's Purse Christmas shoeboxes. I was reminded of the Old Testament book of Isaiah which says, *"For as the rain and snow come down from heaven, and do not return there until they have watered the earth, making it bring forth and sprout, giving seed to the sower and bread to the eater, so shall my word be that goes out from my mouth; it shall not return to me empty, but it shall accomplish that which I purpose, and succeed in the thing for which I sent it"* (Isaiah 55:10-11). God will indeed use His Word to touch hearts and lives, and we were merely the instruments He used that night to get it in people's hands – even if it was just one pair of hands. God always accomplishes His purposes, despite the actions of people. Are we open to God's call and purposes, even when we feel discouraged?

We had a few interesting conversations with some people at the fair, and we had some people ignore us, but the comment that made us the most happy was when a young boy accepted a Testament, and with great excitement, said, "I love this Bible!" That comment and enthusiasm made our day! Jesus loves children, and I think He also loves their enthusiasm, which we sometimes lose as adults. Jesus told His disciples, "*Allow the little children come to Me, and do not hinder them; for to the childlike belongs the kingdom of God. Truly, I say to you, Whosoever shall not receive, as a little child the kingdom of God, they shall not never enter the kingdom*" (Mark 10:14-15). Children are generally innocent, trusting, and enthusiastic, like this boy at the fair was when he was handed a New Testament. As adults, we often lose these wonderful qualities, but Jesus is calling us back to them. The apostle Paul said that we are children of God, and that, "*God has sent the Spirit of his Son into your hearts, crying, Abba! Father. Wherefore you are no longer a servant, but a child, and if a child then also an heir of God through Christ*" (Galatians 4:6-7).

Being a child of God is outrageously exciting! As children of God, we should surely be enthusiastic that we have the greatest Dad of all! He wants to use us to spread the Gospel of His love with joy and excitement. He wants us to pick up a Bible and say, "I love this Bible," because it is God's way of communicating with us. God wants us to ingest His words into our souls. With those words of love and grace that we read in the Bible, we should have great enthusiasm to share them with everyone God places before us. Each morning when I read my Bible, I pray that when I pick up that Great Book, I too will say, "I love this Bible!"

God and Nature

"*Then God said, 'Let there be light'; and there was light*" (Genesis 1:3); this was a verse I thought about as I watched a total solar eclipse last year. With a word, God spoke all things into existence. His creation is amazing – but what is truly amazing, is when God's creation does something spectacular. I traveled several hours to see the totality of a full solar eclipse, and mere words cannot describe this amazing experience. With just a tiny sliver left of the sun, as the moon began to cover the sun, there was still daylight, though a quiet, eerie silence surrounded us as the winds ceased and the birds stopped chirping. Suddenly, as if God hit the switch, there was darkness. A few stars twinkled as the moon completely covered the sun. Only the corona, the beams of the sun, still shone brightly behind the darkened moon. My family was with me as we watched this spectacular event together, and as we all laughed with excitement and stood in amazement at what we were watching, we began to say things like, "Is this what looking at the face of God will be like: too bright to look into?" In describing the New Jerusalem when Jesus someday returns and takes His children home, Revelation 21:23 says, "And t*he city had no need of the sun, neither of the moon to shine in it: for the glory of God did illuminate it, and the Lamb is the lamp therof.*" God continuously displays His glory in His creation, if we would just take the time to reflect and give the praise due to Him. What an awesome God we serve!

For two minutes we could look directly into the fully eclipsed sun without our special glasses, and during that brief amount of time when it was dark, when the sun was still behind the moon, we knew that in just two minutes it would be daylight again. That special moment of the full solar eclipse would not last long at all, but would be all too brief. I thought of the verse in John that says, "*And the Light continues to shine and the darkness could not restrain it*" (John 1:5). Darkness cannot hide the light for long. God's light and love is far greater than the darkness of the enemy – Satan. Jesus said, "*I am the light of the world: he who follows Me will not walk in darkness but will have the light of life*" (John 8:12). I am so grateful that we do not have to stumble in the dark, but when we look to the True Light of the world, we can have perfect direction and guidance in this life. Why would anyone not want that? I also thought about people who do not even believe in the existence of God, which, when looking at creation, baffles me. God said, "I form light and create darkness, I bring prosperity and create disaster; I the Lord, do all these things" (Isaiah 45:7). When the ordinary cycle of day and night is interrupted, as in a total solar eclipse, we still know that God is always in full control of His universe.

Our life here on earth is like the eclipse. For a while there is darkness, like in the total eclipse, but Jesus called us to be "*the light of the world*" (Matthew 5:14), and to show the beautiful love of Jesus in a sin-filled darkened world. We are to be that shining corona behind the darkness of sin. How can we be the light that Jesus spoke about? The prophet Isaiah wrote, "*If you do away with the yoke of oppression, with the pointing finger and malicious talk, and if you spend yourselves in behalf of the hungry and satisfy the needs of the oppressed, then your light will rise in the darkness, and your night will become like the noonday*" (Isaiah 58:9b-10). Darkness covered the noonday sun during the eclipse, and just as that event was opposite of what is the norm, so too, we are to be different from the rest of this world by shining the love of God in the dark places on this earth.

The Mind of Christ

In a blog written by Nicholas Carr, recorded in his book, *Utopia is Creepy*, he wrote that Google hopes to use technology someday that would allow people actually just to think of something, and our friends would be able to experience our thoughts. In other words, people would basically be able to read one another's minds. Who would want that capability? We all struggle with sin, especially in our minds, which is where sin begins. Paul wrote to the Roman Christians, "*And be not fashioned according to this age: but be transformed by a new mental attitude, that you may confirm for yourselves what is good, acceptable, and the complete will of God*" (Romans 12:2). Our natural, human, sinful nature more often than we may care to admit, has sinful thoughts, and our minds do indeed need to be renewed daily by the power of the Holy Spirit. Each day we need to pray for a transforming and renewing of our minds, but we will always struggle in this earthly life.

In the Sermon on the Mount as recorded in Matthew 5, 6, &7, Jesus spoke about the struggles we have in our thought-lives. In Matthew chapter 5, Jesus said if we hate someone, we are guilty of murder. He said if we look upon a person with lust, we are guilty of adultery. Coveting, which many of us do whenever we desire something we do not have which someone else may have, is sin and one of the Ten Commandments, "*Thou shalt not covet*" (Exodus 20:17). Coveting is a sin of the mind, not an action, just as anger, hatred and lust, and Jesus sternly condemns all of these sinful thoughts. If one of those thoughts were in your mind, would you want others to know? Our minds need to be fixed on God. Jesus also said the greatest commandment is to "*Love your God with all your heart, and with all your soul, and with all your mind"* (Matthew 22:37). Our minds need a daily focus on God and His Word.

Unfortunately, we struggle with sin every day in our minds, so who would want others to know our thoughts, as Google hopes one day to make possible? God however, does indeed know all of our thoughts, for which we must often repent. When sinful thoughts do creep into our minds, do we allow ourselves to remain in those thoughts, which often lead us to sinful actions? When a sinful thought enters our minds, do we turn to Christ for help? II Corinthians 10:5 says, *"We demolish arguments and every pretension that sets itself up against the knowledge of God, and we take captive every thought to make it obedient to Christ."* Do we take everything we think of to Christ? Do we long to be obedient to Christ and follow His example? Does Christ captivate every part of our minds, or do we leave some areas of our thought lives to ourselves (or at least think we do). There is a beautiful portion of Scripture I would like to leave with you to meditate on this week, which does indeed assist us in taking every thought captive: *"Finally, brothers, whatever is true, whatever is noble, whatever is right, whatever is pure, whatever is lovely, whatever is admirable – if anything is excellent or praiseworthy – think about such things."* (Philippians 4:8).

How Big is Your God?

Lately in our Wednesday evening service here at the Rescue Mission, we have periodically asked the question, "What keeps us from doing what God wants us to do?" One of the answers was simply our view of God, making Him smaller than He really is, putting God in a box, and not fully realizing the immensity of God. As finite humans, we will never appreciate or grasp just how infinitely large God is, but we should stop shrinking Him as we often do, limiting what we think He is capable of doing. Our faith in God depends not only on what we know of His attributes, such as love, compassion, mercy, forgiveness, righteousness, and justice, but also on just how truly big we perceive Him. We often quote things like, *"with God, all things are possible"* (Matthew 19:26), but do we really believe that?

I have had the privilege of traveling through most of this beautiful country, as well as several other countries. I often paused to contemplate the vastness of God. God knows each and every section of this small part of His creation, the entire earth, and also our gigantic universe of which we cannot even fathom. Psalm 95:3-5 says, *"For the Lord is a great God, and a King above all gods. In his hand are the depths of all the earth; the heights of the mountains are his also. The sea is his, for he made it, and the dry land, which his hands have formed."* In thinking about our world, I am also reminded about the last section of the Wisdom book of Job, when God spoke out of the whirlwind to Job. When Job complained about his life, God questioned him as to where he was when creation was occurring, and if Job could even begin to grasp the immenseness of the universe, let alone the mind of God. Not only does God know every corner of His creation, but He also knows each human being, better than we even know ourselves, and Scripture says He even knows the number of hairs on our head! (Matthew 10:30 & Luke 12"17).

If we serve a God who can create beyond our comprehension, who has no limits, who has no beginning and no end, and who can raise the dead, and who knows literally everything, why do we not trust Him to do the impossible in our lives, or for that matter, merely to provide for us as we need? Why do we continually shrink God? Deuteronomy tells us, *"For the Lord your God is God of gods and Lord of lords, the great God, mighty and awesome"* (Deuteronomy 10:17). How big is God to you? Surely He is big enough to care for you, protect you, and guide you through the life He has lovingly given you. We merely need to trust Him completely, knowing He is far greater, far more powerful, and more perfect in wisdom than we can even begin to imagine. Our God is omniscient (He knows everything), He is omnipresent (He is everywhere at the same time), and He is omnipotent (all-powerful – nothing He cannot do). There is nothing we cannot trust Him to take care of, and because He is also all-loving and perfectly good, He will work all things out for us in perfect love. May you find peace in the arms of our awesome Heavenly Father.

When Life is Hard

Some days are just plain hard. Christians are not immune to pain and suffering, and periodically we live in the reality of that pain. There may be sickness, dying, and death in our families. Maybe there are relational problems that cause us grief, or financial difficulties. Perhaps we are watching a family member struggle in some way which saddens us. I am sure there are many days some of us come to work with concerns, and dare I say even worries? Through the pain, we come to the Mission with smiles on our faces and minister to our clients who are facing very real pain and difficulties in their lives, some problems of which we can relate, other problems of which perhaps we cannot. In order to minister to people in prayer, active listening, and counsel, we must absorb some of their pain, while hiding our own, giving 110% of ourselves in our Christian love for those God brings through our doors. We must push aside ourselves in the care of others, which is not always easy. A former hospice chaplain colleague of mine once told me that when he arrived at a patient's home, he would intentionally slam the car door, reminding himself to leave all of his "stuff" behind so that he could focus on those to whom he was called to serve.

Fortunately, I am reminded of one of my favorite verses in Scripture that speaks of God's profound comfort that is available to us: *"Come to me, all you who are weary and burdened, and I will give you rest. Take my yoke upon you and learn from me, for I am humble and gentle in heart, and you will find rest for your souls. For my yoke is easy and my burden is light"* (Matthew 11:28-30). What is so striking in this passage is that our Mighty God and Creator, is also *"humble and gentle in heart.*" While we remain strong and passionate for God's Word and the Truth of the Gospel, we too are called to be gentle and humble in heart. Do others see that in us? The apostle Paul said, "*Let your gentleness be known to everyone*" (Philippians 4:5).

One of my favorite contemporary Christian songs is by a band called Third Day; their song is entitled, "Cry Out to Jesus." The chorus of the song says, "*There is hope for the hopeless, rest for the weary, and love for the broken heart. There is grace and forgiveness, mercy and healing, He'll meet you wherever you are, cry out to Jesus.*" Jesus is indeed always there for us, to strengthen and heal us in ways that are impossible on our own. If you are having a difficult day, for whatever reason, or you listen to clients who are really struggling, remember to cry out to Jesus, and remind others of that opportunity, as He does indeed comfort us with His mercy and grace, and whose love stretches not only around us, but around the whole world

Praises in the Storm

I once saw a movie called, "*The Insanity of God.*" A portion of that movie told the story about a Russian Christian living under Communist rule, who was imprisoned for his faith. This man started a small house church that grew rather quickly, which the authorities could no longer ignore. He was arrested and sent to a prison that housed hardened and dangerous criminals such as murderers; certainly no place for a gentle man of faith. Each morning this new prisoner stepped out of his cell, raised his arms in praise to his Lord and Savior Jesus Christ, and sang a beautiful hymn of praise. Each morning as he sang in worship, the other prisoners screamed at him, taunted him, and threw things at him, including their own feces. Morning worship continued each and every day, despite the torment he received from his fellow prisoners. The guards of the prison also beat him for this act of worship, yet even that did not stop him.

After years in prison, and years of continuing to praise God in morning worship through this song, the guards took him out of his cell to torture him to death, informing him that within twenty minutes, he would be dead. As he was taken out of his cell, a truly amazing and miraculous thing happened: all of the other prisoners, as they stepped out of their cell for the morning, also lifted their arms and sang this same hymn of praise to God. The guards were terrified and shocked. The power of God, through praise, filled that prison. The guards, in fear, released the man, rather than kill him.

Our initial reaction to difficulties, especially extreme difficulties such as imprisonment, beatings and torture, is certainly not praise to a God who some of us may believe has abandoned us; but, that is what we are called to do. When the apostle Paul and Silas were in prison, they too sang praises to God. Acts 16:23-27 records this event: "*After a brutal flogging they were cast into prison, and gave the jailors orders to guard them securely: receiving such a strict order, the jailor put them in the inner dungeon and secured their feet with stocks. At midnight Paul and Silas prayed and sang praises to God: and the prisoners heard them. Suddenly there was a violent earthquake that shook the foundations of the prison: and once all the doors were opened and everyone's bands were loosed.*" History seems to repeat itself.

God does indeed inhabit the praises of His people, and He performs miracles when do not give up, and when we continue to praise Him, even in the worst storms of life. Do we praise God only when things go well and our prayers are answered as we feel they should be answered? Do we praise God when life is at its absolute worst, such as it was at that time for Paul, Silas, and this Russian prisoner? Of course, it is not in our human nature to praise God in the storms, but we must pray that, through the power of the Holy Spirit, God will enable us to praise Him – no matter what.

Let Go

There is a tribe of people in the remote Pacific islands who regularly eat monkey meat. They have a very easy way of "hunting" the monkeys: they either have a cage with a banana inside or a cut-out log with peanuts to attract the monkeys. The monkeys put their hand in the cage to grab the banana, or into the log to pull out the peanuts, and the men hiding in the bushes simply come out and club the monkeys to death, then eat them for dinner. The strange thing is, the monkeys always see the men coming towards them and panic, yet they refuse to let go of the food. If the monkeys just let go of the peanuts or bananas, they could very easily slip their hands out and run away; the problem is, they will not let go!

We are not much different than these monkeys in the sense that God calls us to let go of many things, including our very selves and our desires, in order to receive all of His abundant blessings and new life in Christ, but we clutch the things of this world that mean so very little. We hold on to our security, our possessions, our homes, even our careers, when sometimes God is calling us to let go and move on to something else He wants for us or somewhere else He desires for us to live. We simply do not want to let go of the perceived control we think we have over our lives.

Many of us can quote Galatians 2:20 which says, "*I was crucified with Christ; nevertheless I live, yet not I, but Christ lives in me: and the life I now live in the flesh I live by the faith of the Son of God, who loved me and gave Himself for me.*" Unfortunately, we have not really crucified ourselves when we will not let go to the things of this world, even at God's command. The great theologian Dietrich Bonhoeffer wrote in his amazing book, *The Cost of Discipleship*, "When Christ calls someone, He bids them, 'Come and die with Me.'" True Christian discipleship is 100% surrender to Christ, and 100% letting go of whatever banana or peanut to which we cling. We must die to ourselves in order to receive new life in Christ. Colossians 3:9-10 says that we have put off the old self, and put on the new self, but we can only do that if we allow the old self to die. I once had a seminary professor say, "If you have truly died…then die!"

Romans 14:7-9 says, "*No one lives or dies to himself. For whether we live or die, we belong to the Lord. For this purpose, Christ both died and arose to life, that He might be Lord of the living and the dead.*" Are we truly the Lord's, or are we still our own? Are we still clinging to the banana or the peanuts that entrap us in this world, when all we need to do is let go and allow God to work out His plans for us in this life, preparing us for the life to come in His kingdom? I would rather not get clubbed over the head before I learn to die to self! May we focus on Christ and Him crucified each day, submitting ourselves to His will, and break free from the entrapments of this world.

Be Still

When Moses led the Israelites out of slavery in Egypt, they encountered a seemingly impossible difficulty: the Red Sea. They had nowhere to go, and as they wondered, in terror what to do, they, *"looked up, and there were the Egyptians, marching after them. They were terrified and cried out to the Lord"* (Exodus 14:10). The Israelites fearfully complained to Moses about their frightening situation. Moses wisely answered them saying, *"Do not be afraid. Stand firm and you will see the deliverance the Lord will bring you today. The Egyptians you see today you will never see again. The Lord will fight for you; you need only be still"* (Exodus 14:13, 14).

How do we respond when we see trouble all around us? The Israelites had the Red Sea in front of them, and Pharaoh's army behind them. Where would they turn? There was literally nowhere to turn *but* to the Lord. What did the Lord do? He made a way of escape for His people by bringing a strong east wind that drove the sea back enough for the Israelites to cross over to the other side. When the Egyptian's tried to cross, their chariot wheels get stuck in the mud, the Egyptian soldiers were confused and got lost in the darkness, and ultimately had the waters of the sea close in around them and destroyed the Egyptian army.

There are often times in our lives when we can only see trouble closing in around us, and, like the Israelites, we panic. If we move forward, in our minds we are doomed. When we look behind us, there is nothing but trouble, fear, and heartache. Sometimes we complain like the Israelites, who told Moses several times that they would have rather remained as slaves in Egypt than take this dangerous journey to the Promised Land.

We are no different than these fearful Israelites. Sometimes God moves us out of our comfort zones – our hometown, our job, maybe even our own country. When circumstances become difficult, challenging, maybe even frightening, we complain and want to turn back, rather than move forward to where God is leading. It is at this point that we must remember that, "*The Lord will fight for you; you need only be still*" (Exodus 14:14). God does not require our help. Sometimes all we need to do is stay right where we are and wait on God, who will part our own Red Sea when needed, and bring us safely to where we need to go. When trouble seems to loom around us from all sides, remember the Exodus: be still, and allow the Lord to fight for you. He is much stronger and wiser than we are, and He already knows what awaits us on the other side of our own Red Sea.

Corporate Worship

Many people in America say they are Christians, but refuse to attend weekly worship services at a local church. While going to church does not make a person a Christian any more than standing in a garage makes someone a car, the Bible does indeed instruct us to gather together in worship. I have heard many arguments as to why people do not attend: the church is full of hypocrites, the services are boring, they are not learning anything new, etc. Some of those arguments and complaints may be true, but let's look at each one, in relation to what the Bible has to say.

Is the church full of hypocrites? Actually, many people in the pews are not even Christians, but are there for social reasons, for business connections, or simply because they attended as a child, became accustomed to going each Sunday, and think it makes them look more respectable. Some of us have also heard the saying that the local church is the "hospital for sinners" where we are hopefully made healthier. What better place for sinners and unbelievers to be than in a worship service where God's Word is proclaimed!

Some churches are more liturgical than others, such as the Lutheran and Episcopal churches. Perhaps if one finds the service boring, there is a need to inquire what the purpose is for the various things done and said in the "Divine Service," so that the service makes more sense. The main focus of the more formal, liturgical services is to corporately partake in the Lord's Supper, hear the Word of God read and preached, and receive God's grace and forgiveness; who amongst us does not need that? Also, the worship service is not about us anyway – it is about praise and worship to our God.

Because many people who attend church services are not literate in the Bible, the messages are often not theologically deep, and the sermons may indeed be review for some Christians. In order to reach the majority of listeners seated in the pews (or chairs) the message cannot be too complicated; that is the purpose of Bible classes and adult Sunday school, where the congregation can indeed delve deeper into Scripture and one can learn more about the Faith.

So why go to church each Sunday? The Bible does indeed tell us to do so. Paul's three pastoral letters, I and II Timothy and Titus gave detailed instructions about corporate worship and church administration, as well as some other books of the Bible. Corporate worship was obviously important to the apostle Paul for him to devote several letters to this topic. Paul also addressed numerous problems that churches had from the very beginning, such as people getting drunk when sharing The Lord's Supper (I Corinthians 11), sexual sins (I Corinthians 5), and divisions and arguments among the church members (I Corinthians 3). There have always been problems in the local churches, and there always will be. I had an Old Testament professor in seminary tell us that, "We will never find the perfect church, because *we* will be in it!" We are all fallen people with sinful natures, but God loves us anyway and desires our corporate praise and worship. The local church is a place where we can hold one another accountable, where we can have extended family, where we can show love and acts of kindness to each other, and where we can pray, read Scripture, take the Lord's Supper, and sing together as they did back in the early Church. The author of Hebrews wrote, "*Let us keep one another in mind, always ready with love and acts of piety, let us not abandon our meeting together, as some habitually do, but let us encourage one another, and all the more as you see the great day drawing near"* (Hebrews 10:24-25).

There are believers in "closed" countries, where it is illegal to gather together for prayer and worship, yet at the cost of imprisonment or even death, underground churches have formed and people gather together for worship. Perhaps they understand much better than some American Christians the power of God and His Holy Spirit when worshipping together. May we too have the passion and understanding of corporate worship, and look forward to our time together on Sunday mornings.

Heal Our Land

Every four years, our country democratically elects a president to lead us. Some people are happy, some people are not. Perhaps we place too much trust in the course of our nation on who we elect. Though our government does indeed decide our policies and laws, according to scripture, our nation's spiritual health plays a much greater role in the course of our country than who we elect. A beautiful and well known verse in the Bible comes from II Chronicles 7:14 which says, *"If my people, who are called by my name, will humble themselves and pray and seek my face and turn from their wicked ways, then will I hear from heaven and will forgive their sin and heal their land."* Do you think our land is in need of any healing? Do we need any restoration in this country in order to continue to receive God's blessings and protection?

It is not a stretch of the imagination to say that our country has indeed veered off course from God's Laws and the path He has laid out for all lands, as recorded in the Bible. While the leaders and founders of our nation were not all Christian (some were, but many were Deists), America was indeed founded on Judeo-Christian principles, with an acknowledgement of God and a healthy respect for the Bible, which is why we still use it in our court rooms. Even though there is a separation of Church and State, meaning the State cannot impose a specific religion or denomination on its people, we do still have a foundation as a nation that feared, trusted, and respected God. Our money does still say, "In God we trust." Fortunately, we still have the freedom to worship, to assemble, and to pray, which many countries do not.

Unfortunately, we have deep divisions in our land: Left vs. Right, Republican vs Democrat, Christian vs. non-Christian, black vs white, etc. We need healing and restoration. The restoration of our country will only come through humility, repentance, and a healthy fear of God, and not in whether we have a Republican or Democrat in office. II Chronicles 7:14 was true in Solomon's day, and is still true today.

When Moses led the Israelites to the Promised Land, he told them, "*Walk in all the way that the Lord your God has commanded you, so that you may live and prosper and prolong your days…*" (Deuteronomy 5:33). We are one of the most prosperous nations in the world, if not *the* most prosperous, and we enjoy a standard of living that most people in the world do not experience. Proverbs 14:34 says, "*Righteousness exalts a nation, but sin is a disgrace to any people.*" We need to turn from our sins of division and of forgetting God.

Psalm 33:12 says, "*Blessed is the nation whose God is the Lord.*" Unfortunately, God is not currently the Lord of our country, but we have made *ourselves* Lord. While still holding to the separation of Church and State, we as Believers in Jesus Christ can live in such a way that our country takes notice of the love we have for one another, the divisions we long to heal, the respect we show one another (even when we sharply disagree), the humility we show, and the trust we have in God to truly heal our land.

A Look in the Mirror

Most of us look in the mirror at some point during the day. The mirror obviously reflects what we look like physically, but do we stop to think that how we spend our time and what we put our efforts into reflect who we really are and what is important to us? How much time do we spend in the mirror thinking about our physical appearance compared to the time we look into the mirror of our souls and reflect on our inward appearance? What are our priorities when it comes to our outward appearance versus our spiritual, inward self as we are called to reflect Jesus Christ? How we choose to spend our time, where our passions lie, and where we expend our energies all reflect who we really are – beyond outward appearances. Do we spend more time reading the newspaper, on-line stories and social media, or watching television than we do reading the Bible? Do we spend more time on entertaining ourselves than we do in worship, fellowship, evangelism, and quiet time with our Lord? What kind of balance do we have in these areas? What do we see when we look into the mirror of our souls, and who do others see when they look at us? When others look at us, do they know we are Christ followers? How can they tell?

I think of the Scripture in the book of James that says, *"For if any are hearers of the word, and not doers, they are like those who look at themselves in a mirror; for they look at themselves and, on going away, immediately forget what they were like. But those who look into the perfect law, the law of liberty, and persevere, being not hearers who forget but doers who act – they will be blessed in their doing"* (James 1:23-25). We can quickly read our morning devotions or passages of Scripture each day, maybe attend worship service on Sunday and feel good about these disciplines, but if we do not spend time learning, studying, praying and seeking the Lord, being doers of His Word rather than just passive hearers of His Word, we do not look any different than unbelievers who live for themselves and for this world. How do we reflect the love of Jesus in our day-to- day lives?

The older we get, perhaps the less time we take looking into the mirror as we lose our youthful appearance; however, our inner selves should be maturing in Christ and in His love and wisdom, which should make us far more attractive than we used to be. We should be growing in beauty inwardly as our souls yearn for more and more of Christ. We need to allow the Holy Spirit to transform our hearts and our minds so that we reflect Him. II Corinthians 3:18 says, *"But we all with unveiled faces, look into polished metal and see ourselves in the mirror of the Lord and are transfigured in ever increasing splendor into the same image from glory to glory, even as by the Spirit of the Lord."* May we all continue to look into the mirror of our inward selves, and see less of ourselves, and more of Jesus.

Alone On the Mountain

Hebrews 11:1 says, "*Now faith is the reality of things hoped for, the proof of things not seen.*" Last week I spoke to a friend who was struggling in his faith; here is why: he is single, and has been all of his life, and is now middle aged. He recently met a woman who he has been dating, who sometimes makes him happy, but basically she only fills in the lonely, empty gap in his life that he longs to have filled with human love. My friend however, is a Christian, and she is not, and he knows this relationship is not of the Lord. When I asked if his walk with the Lord is closer, or if he is falling away because of his girlfriend, he admitted that indeed he was wandering away. Naturally I asked him, "Why don't you break off this relationship?" His response was interesting. He said, "Imagine you have been alone on a mountain for a very long time. You are lonely, tired, cold, and hungry, and you see a helicopter overhead that is dropping off food and blankets. The food is not very good, and the blankets are torn, but it is better than nothing, so you take what you can get. Someone (God) tells you there is much better food on the way, and thick warm blankets, but you do not see or hear another helicopter, and you think it would be crazy to tell this helicopter to fly away and not leave you supplies, just in case there is not another one coming, and who knows if one is indeed on the way, how long it would take? How long do you want to remain cold, hungry, and alone?"

I thought of the story of Abraham and Sarah in Genesis 16 & 17. These two people were old and childless, yet God told Abraham he would be the father of many nations. How could that be, since they had no children, Abraham was very old and Sarah was past childbearing age? The only "helicopter" they saw was Abraham's Egyptian slave girl Hagar, and in their lack of faith of another "helicopter" coming, they decided that Abraham should have a child by Hagar, rather than trust God that somehow, Sarah would indeed have a child as God promised. The result was not good. Sarah threw Hagar and her son Ishmael out, and God was displeased with their disobedience and lack of faith. More than a decade later, Abraham and Sarah did indeed have a son – Isaac, which was the promise of God.

Many of us are just like Abraham and Sarah, and like my friend, who see what appears to be our only option, even when we know God has said otherwise, and we take matters into our own hands, in disobedience to God. We see that first helicopter, and doubt that a second one will appear, even when God has told us another one is coming – it just may take much longer than we would like. God is faithful and will always keep His word. 2 Timothy 2:13 says, "*If we are without faith, He remains faithful: He cannot deny Himself.*" Let me repeat - God is always faithful. When we do not see or hear that second helicopter, but we know God said it is coming, let us pray for the faith and patience to wait upon the Lord, who will always come through and fulfill His promises.

Do You Wish to Get Well?

Jesus said to a sick man, "*Do you wish to get well*?"
(John 5:6). Jesus asked a man who had been sick for 38 years
if he wanted to get well as he lay by the pool of Bethesda in
Jerusalem. Jesus also knew that this man had been lying by
this healing pool for a long time, so why would He even ask
him if he wanted to get well – who wouldn't? At first glance,
the question Jesus asked this man appears odd; however, I
have had many similar conversations with people here at the
Mission: "Do you want to get well? Do you want to break free
from your addiction? Do you want to get off the streets? Do
you want a place you can call home? "Do you want to work
and earn a living?" Oddly enough, sometimes (more often than
I would like) the answer is no! Why is that? Do they, and we,
sometimes consciously or unconsciously want to stay stuck in
the pain, the memories, the addictions, and the sickness that
we are in because it is familiar and has even become in a sense
comfortable? Is it simply too much trouble to get well? Can
we even get well on our own? The answer of course, is no, we
cannot. We need Jesus and His healing touch.

Jesus then said to this man at Bethesda after healing him,
"*Behold, you have become well; do not sin anymore, so that
nothing worse happens to you*" (John 5:14). What did Jesus
mean by that statement? Most of us realize that the longer we
live in our sinful states, the worse life may become since we
are outside of the parameters of God that He set for our own
good and protection. Last week I spoke to a man who was in
tears in the lunch room, who said he was tired of living on the

streets. I knew this man pretty well, and when I pressed him about what occurred in his life that put him on the streets, and more so, what kept him on the streets, he admitted that it was a substance abuse addiction that he simply was not ready to give up, and that he did not look to Jesus for help. I basically asked him if he wanted to get well, and oddly enough, his answer was no. I asked if he wanted Jesus in his life, but he was not ready, and again, his answer was no. Sad. I often speak to many other people in that same situation – tired of being homeless, tired of struggling, and when I ask them if they want a job to enable them to have a roof over their heads, if they want to get well, if they want Jesus, they too sometimes say no.

Jesus came to heal us and continually asks us if we wish to get well, just like the man at the pool in Bethesda. In speaking prophetically about Jesus, Isaiah 53:5 says, "*But He was wounded for our iniquities; upon Him was the punishment that made us whole, and by His bruises we are healed.*" Jesus wants to heal us from all of our diseases, our addictions, our painful memories, our struggles, and to make us whole, but He asks us, "Do we want to be made well?" Only through and in Him, can we truly be made well. May we offer that hope to all those of whom Jesus brings our way, and ask each person, "Do you wish to get well?"

Power

Listening to the news, many people realize we live in a rather volatile and dangerous world. There are terror attacks around the globe, leaving people unsure when and where the next attack will strike. There are threats of nuclear war. I hear many people say the end must be near, and it may be, though people have been saying that for 2000 years, and Jesus has not yet returned. Instead of being held captive to fear, we must remember the magnificent power of our Savior. It seems that throughout the Gospels, Jesus more or less said to those around Him, "Watch this" in order to give a glimpse of the power of our God. Remember when Jesus fed the crowds of thousands on several occasions with just a few fish and loaves of bread – with food leftover? (Mark 6 & 8).

What about during the storm when His disciples were at sea, and even though they were seasoned fisherman, they were frightened by the storm. What did Jesus do? He came to them, walking on the water! Jesus was allowing His closest friends to see that He is Lord over everything – storms, nature, indeed over all of His creation, yet He is always within reach (Mark 6:47- 52 & Matthew 14:22-32). When Peter saw Jesus walking on the water, he said, "*Tell me to come to you on the water*" (Matthew 14:28). When Jesus said, "*Come*" to Peter, he got out of the boat and walked on the water towards Jesus! How often do we tell Jesus that we will do the impossible at His mere command? Jesus has power over all of creation; we only need the faith to believe. The story goes on to say, "*And when they climbed into the boat, the wind died down*" (Matthew 14:32). When Jesus simply stepped into the disciples' boat, the waves ceased and the storm ended. Just the powerful presence of Jesus calms our storms.

The world appears to be in the midst of a massive storm with all that is occurring. In faith, like Peter, we need to step out into the impossible and walk to Jesus, in the midst of the storms, then let Him into our lives (boat) so that He can bring peace, and calm the storms gathering around us. When Peter was walking on the water towards Jesus and realized that this feat was not supposed to be possible, and then looked at the reality of his situation, he panicked and began to sink. Jesus however, reached out to Peter and brought him up safely and said, "*You of little faith, why did you doubt?*" (Matthew 14:31). Jesus did not chastise Peter and watch him sink, but He, "immediately reached out His hand and caught him" (Matthew 14:31). Jesus does the same for us when we call out to Him as we sink in the middle of our own storms. He is always within reach.

The world is a fallen, sinful, broken place, but God is still on the throne, and nothing will happen that He is unaware of or that is outside of His permissive will. The winds and the waves obeyed Jesus. He did the impossible and also allowed Peter to do the impossible by walking on water. He is still in the business of the impossible. When Jesus' disciples witnessed all they had just seen, they said, "*Truly you are the Son of God*" (Matthew 14:33b).

There are mighty acts of God's powers all around us, every day, if we stop to take notice. In the book of Job, God spoke of His power, "*out of the storm*" (Job 40:6) when He mentioned the vastness and greatness of His creation, of which Jesus proved He was Master, such as walking on the water and calming the storm with His words. Creation was brought into existence by the words of God as well. Job understood God's power, as did

Jesus' disciples, when he replied to God, *"I know you can do all things; no plan of yours can be thwarted"* (Job 42:2). Nothing will ever happen here on earth without the knowledge and consent of God. We need not fear the storms, the winds, the crashing waves, but reach out to Jesus, the power of God, and at His command, like Peter, do the impossible.

Prayer

Last week at our staff meeting, we spoke about a very important topic: prayer. There were many very thoughtful comments made about prayer, which included: prayer as a spiritual discipline (that is not always easy to adhere to), prayer as a means to communicate with God our deepest desires and longings, prayer as a means to draw close to God and share an intimate relationship with Him, and prayer as a way to intercede and pray for the needs of others, to name a few. James 5:16 instructs us to pray for one another, which is a way to love each other. Jesus taught His disciples, and us, how to pray with what we call "*The Lord's Prayer*" as found in Matthew 6:9-13. This prayer tells us to honor God, to submit to His will, to petition Him for our daily needs, to ask for forgiveness and also commands us to forgive others, to ask God to stay near us, protect us, and to strengthen us.

"Prayer changes things" is a common statement, of which I agree, but I respectively add, "Prayer changes people." Prayer causes us to press in to God, to desire a relationship with Him, and to always keep Him in the forefront and center of our lives. My five year old granddaughter used to go to a Christian pre-school in a church building, but now attends kindergarten at a public school. She came home on her first day of school and told her parents that almost no one prayed before they ate their lunch, which surprised her. The simple faith of a child is beautiful. Despite most of the other children not praying, my granddaughter continues to pray before she eats her lunch – just a simple thank you, knowing all she has is from Jesus. Prayer is also a form of gratitude.

The apostle Paul said to, "*Pray without ceasing*" (I Thessalonians 5:17). What does that mean? Obviously we cannot pray 24/7, so it must be more of a state of being – a way of life. There is a beautiful little book written by brother Lawrence entitled, "*The Practice of the Presence of GOD*," which talks about having the mindfulness of God's presence with us at all times, which is basically the discipline of praying without ceasing. Brother Lawrence wrote in his book, "The presence of God is the concentration of the soul's attention on God, remembering that He is always present… a reality that becomes natural." Brother Lawrence also said, "The most effective way for communicating with God was to simply do his ordinary work …out of a pure love for God… and believed it was a serious mistake to think of our prayer time as being different than any other" (p. 23). I pray to have that same attitude of prayer that Brother Lawrence had, and as St. Paul said, to "pray without ceasing," and for prayer to be a natural part of my daily life.

A Battle of the Will

Many of us, myself definitely included, have ideas about our lives such as where we will live, what kind of work we will do, if we will get married and have children, etc. Of course there is nothing intrinsically wrong with making plans, preparing ourselves educationally for careers, and having dreams, but we must always remember that God is ultimately in control of all of these things in our lives, and we must submit to His will in everything. Perhaps one of the most difficult things in life is this battle of our will – wanting things our own way, and not surrendering our will to God and His way. I had an old pastor friend who knew my stubbornness, and used to say to me, "You can do what you want and fight God all you want, but just remember in the end, who will win!" Needless to say, I always lost.

Jesus submitted His will to God the Father all the way to death on the Cross. When He was in the Garden of Gethsemane, knowing what He was about to face, in anguish Jesus said, "*Abba, Father, all things are possible for you; spare Me this cup: nevertheless, not My will, but your will*" (Mark 14:36). Jesus was totally submitted to God and put His own will aside in order to live out the call on His life, which was to reconcile us to God through His atoning death on the Cross. Our human nature wants what WE want, or what we think we want, and does not naturally submit to our Father like Jesus did. When we fight (or try to fight) God, we are out of His will and may miss out on the purposes God has for our lives. The apostle Paul knew what he was put on this earth for, and even when he knew he faced grave danger, he pushed forward, doing what he knew was God's will for his life. In the book of Acts, chapter

20, Paul said that he was "*compelled by the Spirit*" to go to Jerusalem, "*not knowing what will happen there: except that the Holy Spirit bears witness in every city, that bonds and afflictions await me. But none of these things move me, neither count I my life of value to myself, so that I might finish my course with joy, and the ministry that I received from the Lord Jesus, to witness the gospel of the grace of God*"(Acts 20:22-24). In Acts chapter 21, the prophet Agabus predicted that Paul would be bound in chains and delivered over to people who hated him if he went to Jerusalem. His friends urged him not to go, but Paul believed God wanted him to go to Jerusalem, so he insisted that, "*The Lord's will be done*" (Acts 21:14). Like Paul, we are called to follow the Lord's will, even if it leads us to our deaths; this is where the battle of wills often arises.

We were all put on this earth for a purpose, but if we do not ask for God's guidance and for the Holy Spirit to enable us to hear His voice and follow His commands, we will miss out on the joy of knowing that we are living out the call God placed on our lives. Paul had a very fruitful ministry, preaching the Gospel to many people in many lands, teaching the way of Jesus Christ. Paul was the first great missionary of whom many have since tried to emulate. Like Paul, some of us are called to the mission field, some are called to other types of ministry, and some are called to secular work, but we are all called to be a witness of Jesus Christ and to spread His love and the Gospel of salvation in Christ alone wherever God chooses to place us. May we indeed be found in the center of His will.

Only One Life

When I was a child, I remember a plaque that hung in our house which said, *"Only one life 'twill soon be past, only what's done for Christ will last."* Only recently did I learn that was written by a missionary and pastor named Charles Thomas (C.T.) Studd. Mr. Studd was an English missionary who lived from 1860-1931. C.T. Studd served as a missionary in China, India, and various countries in Africa; he said some other very powerful things during his lifetime, such as, "If Jesus Christ is God and died for me, then no sacrifice can be too great for me to make for Him." Do we feel that same way? Are there sacrifices we make in life that seem too much – even for God (though we would not dare admit that)? How much do we desire to remain in our comfort zones, or to hold tightly to what we have, and resist sacrifices, even those we think God is calling us to make?

Years ago, I traveled to Calcutta, India to serve at the Missionaries of Charity. I felt that if God ever called me to be a missionary in that part of the world, I simply could not; I hate to admit this, but I thought it would be too much of a sacrifice. I did not like Calcutta at all! But what about what C.T Studd said? "No sacrifice can be too great." Maybe God is calling us to move from our home to another state, or even to another country. Maybe God is calling us to begin a new career, a new job, or a new educational program; are we ready and willing to do whatever God says, even at the sacrifice of our own desires and comforts? Do we honestly ever feel that God is calling us to make too much of a sacrifice, such as to go somewhere or do something we may not really wish to do or feel capable of doing? What if God calls us to serve in a dangerous part of the world – would we go? C.T. Studd also once said, "Some wish to live within the sound of a church or a chapel bell; I wish to run a rescue shop within a yard of hell." How do we feel about that bold statement? Scott Gunn, an Episcopal priest, is of a similar mind when he wrote, "Bold risks and brave actions are the stuff of the Gospel. Safety and comfort are not." Is that true? I think of Proverbs 18:10 which says, *"The name of the Lord is a strong tower; the righteous run into it and are safe."* We are truly safe, no matter where, when we run to the Lord. Would we be safe running "a rescue shop within a yard of hell? Is God not also there?

The apostle Paul wrote some beautiful words along these same lines in the book of Romans. He wrote, *"Who shall separate us from the love of Christ? Shall trouble or misfortune, or harassment, or starvation, the absence of clothing, or the threat of danger, or the sword?"… In all these things, I vote no because we are more than conquerors through Him who loves us. For I am convinced, that neither death, nor life, nor messengers from heaven, nor rulers from earth, nor powers, nor things present, nor things to come, not anything above or below, nor any power in the whole of creation, shall be able to separate us from the love of God, which is in Christ Jesus our Lord"* (Romans 8:35 & 37-39). We truly are never separated from the loving arms of our Creator. May our love for God, and our trust in His Word, allow us to live with the thoughts of C.T Studd, and may we be willing to sacrifice whatever God calls us to, knowing we can never be separated from His love.

What's in a Name?

A new client, who has only been coming to the Mission periodically for lunch this past month, attended our Memorial service last week. I spoke with him briefly and told him that I was happy he came. He said when he heard we were having a memorial service he wanted to attend since he has never, "acknowledged" his brother's death in twenty five years, and this enabled him to do so. He said it was important to speak and hear his brother's name, and to merely acknowledge his death. This man's comments made me think about how important it is for us to acknowledge Jesus' death each day, and to speak His name, for there is power in the name of Jesus.

From the very beginning of human history, Genesis 4:26 says, *"People began to invoke the name of the Lord."* King David also wrote, *"And those who know your name put their trust in you"* (Psalm 9:10a). Why can we place our trust in the name of the Lord? Because, *"The name of the Lord is a strong tower; the righteous run into it and are safe"* (Proverbs 18:10). We are safe because of God's perfect love for us and the sacrifice He made because of that love. Jesus told us in the very beginning of the Lord's Prayer, that the name of our Heavenly Father is "hallowed," which means sacred, to set apart as holy, and to consecrate. We must set the name of the Lord apart as holy each day, which is why the third Commandment instructs us not to make wrongful use of the name of God, and take His name in vain. God's name is indeed holy. The ancient Jews would not even speak or write God's name, because it is so holy. There is power in the name of our Lord. The prophet Joel said, *"Everyone who calls on the name of the Lord shall be saved"* (Joel 2:32), and we have that salvation because of Jesus' death and resurrection. The apostle Peter also said, *"No one else can bring salvation: for there is no other name under heaven given among men, whereby we may be saved"* (Acts 4:12). Throughout Scripture we are told to be baptized in Jesus' name to receive the gift of the Holy Spirit (Acts 2:38 for example). Because the name of the Lord is so holy, Jesus said that if we just give someone a cup of cold water and bear His name, we will be rewarded (Mark 14:41). Throughout the New Testament, even demons would flee at the name of Jesus (Acts 19:13-16).

How do we also acknowledge Jesus' death each day? One way is to never take our sins lightly or think they do not really matter. Jesus went to the Cross, suffered horribly, and died for each one of our sins – even those we may think are not very "big." Of course, we cannot earn our way to Heaven, but we can, with the power of the Holy Spirit, attempt to live by the precious Word of God and be a light shining in a darkened world, as we too invoke the name of our Lord and Savior. We acknowledge Jesus' death by understanding the enormity of His sacrifice on our behalf. We acknowledge His death by loving Him completely, because He first loved us. We acknowledge His death by completely surrendering our lives to Him. May we daily speak the beautiful, powerful name of our Savior, Jesus the Christ, and acknowledge the holiness of His name. May we remember His sacrifice for us – death on the Cross.

Fear

Over 100 hundred times in the New Testament, Jesus said, "Fear not" or "Don't be afraid." Why? Does Jesus know how fearful we humans can be at times? Today's world is indeed a frightening place. Floods at record levels, hurricanes stronger than ever... Almost daily we hear of the possibility of nuclear war or hydrogen bombs threatening to destroy much of our country, on-going terrorist attacks in many, many countries around the world. The list seems to go on and on. We seem to be standing at the Red Sea with rising waters in front of us, soldiers behind us, and a fearful scenario all around us. In our postmodern world, do we still hear Jesus say, "Fear not; don't be afraid"? In the Old Testament, we all know what God did for Moses and the Israelite's – He parted the Red Sea for them to cross safely, yet closed the waters and drowned their enemies who pursued them. In the Gospels, Jesus told the leader of the synagogue, "Do not fear, only believe" (Mark 5:36) when he was told that his daughter had died; but what happened next? Jesus raised her from the dead! When it seems that all hope is lost, Jesus walks onto the scene; He did that back then, and He can still do that now. Do we still hear His voice telling us not to fear?

Most of also know Psalm 23 which says, "even though I walk through the valley of the shadow of death, I fear no evil, for you are with me." There is a great amount of evil in this world that surrounds us, yet God told us that we should not fear. Why? Because God truly is with us, and has already conquered death and won the victory over evil when He rose from the dead. I simply cannot imagine living in this chaotic world of evil and not know the strength, the power, and the love of a God who is completely in control, who can part the seas, heal the sick, even raise the dead.

When life runs smoothly, we may not always notice the power of God, but when life is frightening, when we stand at the Red Sea with nowhere to go and face certain death, that is where God works – if we trust Him. One of the saddest verses in the Bible (in my opinion) is Matthew 13:58 which says, "And He (Jesus) did not do many deeds of power there, because of their unbelief." What a tragedy that our unbelief may stop God from performing miracles! Several times in Scripture Jesus was perplexed at the unbelief of even His disciples. When Jesus walked on the water and made the storm cease after He entered His disciple's boat, Scripture said that they were "utterly astounded, for they did not understand about the loaves, but their hearts were hardened" (Mark 6:51&52). Jesus had just finished feeding five thousand people with five loaves of bread and two fish, yet the disciples still had fear. Like us, how quickly they forgot what Jesus was/is capable of doing. In our lack of faith, can our hearts also be hardened? May we always trust our Lord in all circumstances – even as we stand at the Red Sea, unsure of where to go; He will lead us and protect us.

Unexpected People

Last week at our Mission banquet, Ron, our speaker, talked about how Denver, an uneducated, homeless man, changed his life. Ron spoke about how Denver had such great insight and wisdom from whom he learned, even though Ron was an educated, wealthy, and successful man. Like perhaps many of us, especially those of us with good educations and advanced degrees, we tend to think we have the answers and know what is best. We may think, "What could an uneducated, poor person have to teach me?" How wrong and arrogant that type of thinking is on our part. Scripture says that, "*but God has chosen the average to bewilder the wise; and God has chosen the weak things of the world to amaze the strong; and the poor of the world, and the insignificant, hath God chosen, and God gave an affirmative vote to things which are not, to bring to naught things that are: that no human pride could boast in His presence*" (I Corinthians 1:27-29). Do we ever boast in our positions, educations, or status in society? If we have, how has God humbled us, and who has He brought into our lives to teach us? Probably, like Ron, some very unexpected people.

The prophet Isaiah wrote concerning God, "*My thoughts are not your thoughts, nor are your ways My ways, says the Lord. For as the heavens are higher than the earth, so are My ways higher that your ways, and My thoughts than your thoughts*" (Isaiah 55:8-9).Some of our most profound learning does not always take place in the college classroom, but God deliberately places unexpected people in our lives to teach us His wisdom, if we open our minds and hearts to them and to the wisdom God freely wants to give to us.

The apostle Paul also gave us an example of God using the "*low and despised in the world*" to teach us and to show us

just how important all people are in His sight. In the book of
Philemon, Paul met a runaway slave named Onesimus while he
was in prison. Slaves have never been viewed in a positive light,
just as homeless people; yet, Paul called Onesimus his "*child*"
(verse 10) and said he was "*indeed useful*" (verse 11) to him and
was "*of service to him during his imprisonment*" (verses 10-13).
Paul did not view Onesimus as a slave, but rather as a "*beloved
brother*" (verse 16). Of course we do not have slaves anymore
(thank God!), but we can learn a great deal from the apostle
Paul, and from our speaker Ron and his friend Denver, about
how we need to view those people who come to us each day –
the homeless, the addicts, the poor, the uneducated, etc. Do we
view them as our brothers and sisters? Do we think they can
be useful to us in that God may teach us things through them,
or that they may be of a benefit to us and to our ministries?
In their book, *Same Kind of Different as Me* (written by Ron
and Denver), Denver said, "I hope people will recycle the love
they've been given to somebody that's not easy to love" (p.
242), and that it was the love he received from Ron's wife, Miss
Debbie, "that caused him to want to change his life" (244). Ron
wrote that when we look at homeless people, that we need, "to
see through the rags and filth into the person's heart" (242).
May we be mindful of all of the people God places in our paths,
and open to hearing the wisdom of God-perhaps in the most
unexpected places.

Grace Abounds

This morning as I listened to the news, I heard a short interview with a Catholic priest, Father Jonathan Morris, concerning the recent shooting at a church in a small Texas town that resulted in 26 deaths. Shock, outrage, anger, fear, confusion: these are some of the emotions people deal with in times such as this horrific tragedy. One of the newscasters asked Father Morris, "Where is God in this?" Father Morris responded that God is right there in the midst of this massacre, grieving with us, and extending His love in the presence of evil, of which free will does (unfortunately) allow. Many great thinkers throughout the ages have grappled with the concept of absolute evil (Satan) and absolute good (God) with various different theologies and philosophies. As Christians, we know that such absolutes do indeed exist. Father Morris went on to say that, yes, "Evil exists, but grace abounds."

When I heard Father Morris' comment on the news, I thought of Romans 5:20-21, which says, *"But where sin flourished, grace flourished much more: and sin had the power of death even so might grace have the power through righteousness unto eternal life by Jesus Christ our Lord."* Father Morris joined in the mourning of those who died, especially for the children and young people, but said he, as all Christians, have the assurance of eternal life in Heaven with our Lord; that is what we hold on to in times such as this. I also heard that the few remaining people of the church, who were not killed, along with the rest of the small community which was greatly impacted by this tragedy, remained "steadfast in the faith."

If this evil happened in your church or mine, and our children, grandchildren, and maybe all of our family members were killed, would we remain steadfast in our faith? Would we have questions, doubts, fears? What would be our prayer? Would there seem to be a reason, or would these killings appear as random acts of pure evil? How would we answer the question, "Where is God in this?" Would we be able to respond as Job did, when he learned that all of his children were killed, and then, *"fell to the ground and worshiped and said, 'The Lord gave and the Lord has taken away; blessed be the name of the Lord'"* (Job 1:20b & 21b)? What are our questions when we seem to hear day after day of pure evil, random mass shootings, terror attacks, violence, and killings of innocent people just walking down the street or riding their bikes, or even sitting in church worshipping God?

Perhaps Revelation talks about times such as these when it says, *"Woe to the inhabitants of the earth and the sea! Because the devil came down to you, having great anger, because he knows that he has but a short time"* (Revelation 12:12b). It is o.k. to have questions when tragedy strikes, and perhaps to wonder, but we must also remain steadfast in our faith. Now is not the time to turn from God, but to run to Him and to embrace His Word. When many people turned away and no longer followed Jesus, He asked His disciples if they also were going to go away. *"Then Simon Peter answered, 'Lord, to whom shall we go? You have the words of eternal life'"* (John 6:68). Jesus did indeed have the words to eternal life back then, and He still does today. Indeed, where else can we go during such evil and sad times, but to the Words of our Savior, Jesus Christ? May we always be held in His loving embrace, fearing no evil, and knowing He is with us.

Holiness

Holiness is a word we do not use very often here in America and is perhaps a foreign concept to most people. For some people, holiness means following the rules and being "good." However, Jesus said that, "*There is none good but One, that is, God*" (Mark 10:18). God called Himself Holy (Leviticus 11:44), and told people they were on holy ground whenever they were in His presence, such as when God was speaking to Moses; God said, "*Come no closer! Remove the sandals from your feet, for the place on which you are standing is holy ground*" (Exodus 3:5). God gave the Ten Commandments to Moses on Mount Sinai, which was also a holy place because of the presence of God. God told Moses concerning this mountain, "*You shall set limits for the people all around saying, 'Be careful not to go up the mountain or to touch the edge of it. Any who touch the mountain shall be put to death'*" (Exodus 19:12)." In 2 Samuel 6:1-7 and 1 Chronicles 13:9-12, Uzzah and Ahio were driving the cart that carried the Ark of the Covenant. When the oxen shook the cart as they walked, Uzzah, "*put out his hand to hold the ark*" (1 Chronicles 13:9) so it would not fall, and was immediately killed by the hand of the Lord. King David, who was dancing before the ark (which was holy because of the presence of God), naturally became frightened as he witnessed the awesome power and holiness of God.

Well these are just Old Testament stories you may say, but God is the same, yesterday, today, and forever (Hebrews 13:8) and Malachi 3:6 says, "*For I the Lord do not change.*" The God of the Old Testament is the God of the New Testament. The only difference is that when Jesus died and the curtain in the temple to the Holy of Holies was torn from top to bottom

(Mark 15:38), we now have direct access to God, where people once did not. We can go directly to God and ask for forgiveness, whereas in the Old Testament, only a priest, once a year on the Day of Atonement (Leviticus 16), could go into the Holy of Holies and make a sacrifice for himself and for the sins of the people. The priest would even tie bells onto his robe and then tied a rope around himself, in case the holiness of God struck him down and killed him, and the people could drag him out using the rope without entering that most holy of places.

Our American secular culture has co-mingled with our worship and crept into our churches, creating an atmosphere where we no longer view God as Holy, but sometimes as simply our good buddy to whom we can approach in any manner we choose. Proverbs 1:7 says, *"The fear of the Lord is the beginning of knowledge."* We need to have a healthy fear of God's holiness, and approach Him as a holy God. The New Testament book of Acts, chapter 5, tells the story of Ananias and his wife who were both struck down dead for lying to the Holy Spirit. God, in all of His Being - Father, Son, and Holy Spirit, is indeed holy, and should be worshipped as such.

Fortunately, because of God's great love for us, we do serve an approachable, loving, merciful God, and Jesus did call us His *"friends"* (John 15:15), but He is still holy. We should all realize what an amazing privilege it is today, to be able to talk with a holy God, to now have the ability to be in His presence, and to be in a loving, merciful, and forgiving relationship with Him because of what Jesus did for us on the Cross. May we never take that most precious gift that He has given, His very life, and the forgiveness we receive, lightly, and may we always remember God's holiness.

The Waterfall

At our staff retreat we were given a wonderful 45 minutes to meditate on God, anywhere we chose to be, through prayer, meditation, Scripture reading, or by simply being still before the Lord and waiting on Him. It was a crisp, autumn, sunny day, so I decided to take a walk outdoors. As anyone who knows me can tell you, I cannot sit still, and I enjoy praying and meditating while I move, whether it is running or walking. As I walked the grounds, I was drawn to a small path that led into a wooded area. As I walked towards the path, I could hear the sound of rushing water, and came to a spot where I saw a small waterfall, a bridge that went across the water, and water cascading over some large stones. The soothing sound of rippling water assisted my meditation on the goodness and beauty of God and of His creation. I thought of Psalm 46:10 that says, "*Be still, and know that I am God; I will be exalted above the nations, I will be exalted on the earth.*" At this point in time, I was indeed able to "*be still*" in the glory of our God. As I stood on the bridge, watching and listening to the water, I thought of an Old Testament story in I Kings 19:

I Kings 19 tells the story of Elijah who fled from Jezebel, in fear for his life after killing the prophets of Baal. Elijah believed he remained the only follower of God and he was fearful. In exhaustion, he fell asleep under a tree, and an angel of the Lord came to him and brought him some food, which strengthened him. Then the word of the Lord came to him and asked what he was doing, and Elijah responded that the Israelites had rejected God's covenant, killed many prophets, and that they were trying to kill him as well. The Lord instructed Elijah to stand on the mountain in the presence of the Lord, and the Lord would pass by. A great and powerful wind came, but Elijah did not hear the Lord in the wind. An earthquake hit, but the Lord was not heard in the earthquake. Next came a fire, but still the Lord was not heard in the fire. Perhaps though, God was indeed in each manifestation, since He did say that He would *"pass by,"* but Elijah simply did not hear God. Perhaps Elijah simply did not recognize God's glory. Then came a gentle whisper, which Elijah finally heard as the voice of the Lord. God said He would pass by in each event, so was He not there? Why was He not heard?

This story about Elijah came to my mind as I listened to the small waterfall; though not loud, it was the loudest sound out there in the woods. The water rippling over the stones was the next sound I heard, then the quiet, stiller water, and finally, the cool, gentle breeze across my face. In all of these elements of nature, God was indeed there. Do we notice Him? Do we rest in His gentle whisper even when the strong winds of life blow us around, the earthquakes of fear and tragedies hit, the fires of temptation seem to consume us? Do we only hear God in gentle whispers, when life is quiet and calm? Do we only worship during these good and gentle times, or like Job, even in the storms, do we still worship? (Job 1:20). While there are many interpretations to the story of Elijah, I meditated on the part where God said that He would *"pass by,"* and thought about how we must always hear Him, always see His glory, in all circumstances, and always worship. It is easy to worship out in the woods, listening to waterfalls, but I pray I can also worship during the winds, the earthquakes, and the fires as well. Through those tumultuous times, God will indeed speak to us in a gentle whisper, reminding us of His love and faithfulness, and that He is indeed always there, even when we cannot hear.

Words and Actions

Probably all of us at one time or another have experienced disappointment with people who have let us down. How often has someone said they would do something for you, yet failed to live up to their commitment? Does the Bible speak of this experience? Yes. Even God has experienced this with people who say they will follow Him, be obedient to Him, and love Him, yet they failed to do so. There is a parable in Matthew 21:28-32 of two sons. Their father asked the first son if he would work in his vineyard, and this son said no, but later changed his mind and he did indeed go and work. Then the father asked his second son to work in his vineyard, and the son said, "I will, sir," but he did not go. Jesus asked, "'Which of the two sons did what his father wanted?' 'The first' they answered'" (Matthew 21:31). Jesus astonishingly told the high priests and elders of the temple that, "even the tax collectors and harlots will precede you into the kingdom of God" (Matthew 21:31b) because the Pharisees merely paid lip service to God, while living lives that did not reflect His love or their obedience to Him.

While there is deeper theological meaning to this parable than keeping one's word, but rather of who will enter the Kingdom of God, it also is about our hearts, our minds, and our bodies doing what we say we will do, especially in relation to God. In keeping with the theological concept of which this parable was told and recorded in Scripture, we must ask ourselves if we merely give lip service to God, yet do not obey Him or live within the power of His love and grace. Are we like the harlots and the tax collectors who knew they needed the loving forgiveness of a Savior and humbly came before Jesus, or are we rather like than the Pharisees who mistakenly thought they could rely on their own righteousness to enter the Kingdom of God?

As Christ followers, our lives must be lived in humble submission to our Lord, knowing that there is nothing we can do to earn our way into His Kingdom, and that what we profess with our lips, must be lived out in our lives. Matthew 5:37 says, *"But let your words simply be yes or no; for whatever is more than that has its source in evil."* As Christians, we are to be different from the world in many ways: we are to love everyone, including our enemies and those who do not love us, we are to forgive those who hurt and injure us, we are to obey God's commands – no matter the consequences, we are to die to ourselves, and among many other things, we are to be people of our word – to God and to people. We cannot offer righteous lip service to God, yet live far from Him, and neither should we offer lip service to people, yet ignore our commitments. We are to live as honorable people, doing what we say we will do, living as we profess to live through our faith, and being godly people who reflect the character of Christ.

Waiting and Patience

The Gospel of Luke tells the story about an old man named Simeon, who waited all of his life for *"the restoration of Israel: and the Holy Spirit was upon him. And the Holy Spirit revealed to him that he should not see death before he had seen the Lord's Anointed"* (Luke 3:25b-26). Luke said Simeon was a *"righteous and devout man"* (Luke 2:25), yet he waited many, many years, into his old age, to receive what he had waited for all of his life: to see the Messiah. Scripture does not state the age of Simeon, but after holding baby Jesus in his arms, he said he was ready to now, *"depart in peace"* (Luke 2:29), meaning he was now ready to die after seeing Jesus, leaving us to believe he was well advanced in years. Simeon said, *"For my eyes have seen your saving power, that you have prepared before the face of all peoples"* (Luke 230-31). The righteous man Simeon waited his entire life, into old age, to receive from God what he had been waiting for.

There were many strong people of faith in the Bible who had to wait many, many years for their hopes and God's promises to be fulfilled. In the book of Genesis, Abraham and Sarah had to wait until their old age to have their son Isaac. According to Genesis 17:17, Abraham was 100 years old, and Sarah was ninety years old when they finally had the child God had promised. They both laughed in disbelief that God would fulfill His promise to them, since it appeared impossible, but remember that with God, all things are possible! (Matthew 19:26). Have you had to wait a long time for God's promises to be fulfilled, or perhaps you are still waiting, and becoming doubtful. In my own life, I had prayed for a husband for over thirty years, yet God did not fulfill that wish or answer my prayer until I was 53 years old! Like Abraham and Sarah, God works in His own time, which usually is not the same as ours.

Scripture speaks much about patience. Proverbs 19:11 says, "*A person's wisdom yields patience.*" The apostle Paul wrote that in order to walk worthy of the Lord, we must endure much suffering, and be patient for God to fulfill His promises to us and to answer our prayers according to His will, in His time, which is always perfect (Colossians 1:11 & 2 Corinthians 6:6). Is there something you have been praying for, for a long time that has still not come to pass? Do not give up or try to plan things in your own way, outside of God's will like Abraham and Sarah did when they doubted God and Abraham took his slave girl Hagar to have a son, doubting that Sarah could conceive in her old age; all that brought was trouble and discord. God has His plans, in His time, for our best, and He often calls for us to be patient, very patient, maybe to test our faith and our trust in Him. Psalm 40:1&3 says, "*I waited patiently for the Lord; He turned to me and heard my cry...He put a new song in my mouth, a hymn of praise to our God. Many will see and fear the Lord and put their trust in Him.*" When we wait patiently on God to fulfill His perfect plans in His perfect timing, others will see the goodness of God and perhaps also trust Him to fulfill His promises to them, as they too wait in His timing and plan.

We have all heard the phrase, "patience is a virtue" from a 5th century poem; we all know that, yet being patient is often so difficult! Paul wrote, "*But if we hope for that we see not, then do we with enduring patience wait for it*" (Romans 8:25). If you are patiently waiting on God to answer your prayer, remember Abraham and Sarah. Remember me. Remember so many others who waited on God for many, many years, and in your patient waiting, remember others are watching you, seeing your faith as you wait on God's perfect timing, knowing He knows what is best for us, and will act according to His good and perfect will in our lives.

Not Our Own

I have often heard many people use a phrase that I disagree with; they say that God asks us to do things. In the Bible, God calls Himself our Father, and we are His children. For those of us who are parents, when is the last time you asked your children to clean their rooms or do some other household chores? When you were a child, did your parents ask you to do your chores – or did they tell you to do the work they expected to have completed? Children are not normally asked to do anything, but are always told what to do. At the beginning of most of his letters (epistles), the apostle Paul called himself a slave and a bond servant to Jesus Christ. In the ancient world of slavery (and unfortunately even in our modern day where slavery still exists), slaves were never asked to do anything; they were told or commanded to do the work prescribed to them. Slaves had no will of their own, but they simply did what their masters told them to do. If we are God's children, and He is our Father, or if we are His bondservants and He is our Master, He never asks us to do anything; He tells us what to do, and we are expected to obey.

When I mentioned this idea about God never asking us to do something, a friend of mine said, "Well, God does indeed ask us, because we can always say no." When we are told to do something, we always have the option of saying no, like Jonah did when God told him to go to Nineveh as recorded in the book of Jonah. Again, God did not ask Jonah to go – He told him. We still have the freedom to say no when we are told to do something, but sometimes God does not take no for an answer. In the story of Moses in Exodus chapters 3&4, God called Moses to lead the Israelites out of Egypt and into the

Promised Land. Moses had several excuses as to why he could not perform this intimidating task, but God did not ask Moses – He told him he would carry out this task. Moses actually asked God to send someone other than himself to do this, and Scripture said God's *"anger burned against Moses"* (Exodus 4:14). God told Moses what to do, and expected him to do it! As a parent or grandparent, do you not get angry when you tell your kids or grandkids to do something, and they do not do what you said? God is not pleased with our rebellion either. In Exodus 20, when God gave Moses the Ten Commandments, they were just that – commandments, not suggestions. God does indeed tell us what He expects of us and what to do, and He does not ask.

Sometimes though, God tells us to do something or to go somewhere, and utilizing our free will, we say no. God may not force us to do what he said (as He did with Moses), but He may pass over us, find another person to do what He said, and we simply miss out on the blessings He had in store for us had we been obedient. I wonder how many blessings I may have missed out on in my disobedience. Jesus also said that if we love Him, we will obey His commands (John 14:23). Doing what God tells us to do is not burdensome, but is a joy, and in faith, we should realize that His ways are perfect and loving, and what he tells us to do is for our own good and for His glory. May we cheerfully do all God tells us to do each day, receive the blessings He longs to give us, and delight in His perfect will.

Truth

Not long ago I read an article on the Internet that I thought was quite strange. The topic was marriage, and a rather unconventional marriage. The couple was not romantically attracted to one another but felt they were "soul mates" and best friends, so they wanted to marry one another. They will pursue physical intimacy outside of their marriage and have an "open marriage." The young woman from this couple was quoted as saying, "The more we face reality, the more we can see that there is no right or wrong." The article went on to quote producer and assistant director Christopher Ray who said, "Perception is merely reality filtered through the prism of your own soul." Like Ray, society says that we are the definers of truth, but the Bible says much differently: God defines truth, and His Truth is absolute and does not change according to our feelings or situations. Jesus said, "*I am the way, the truth, and the life*" (John 14:6). Truth is not relative; we do not make up the truth as we go along, as our soul tells us, or as our feelings lead us. Our souls and our minds are tainted by sin, which does not allow us to see the Truth clearly without the Holy Spirit. The "prism of our soul" is clouded and sinful. Jeremiah 17:9 says, "*The heart is devious above all else; it is perverse.*" Even Jesus did not entrust Himself to man because "*He knew the nature of men*" (John 2:24). We are lost in our sin without Jesus and His Truth. King David wrote, "*Lead me in your truth, and teach me, for you are the God of my salvation*" (Psalm 25:5). Truth is defined and given to us by God alone, and not of our own making, changing from day to day.

Sometimes the Truth God gives us is not easy to accept, but it is perfect because it is from God. Each year I try to attend the March For Life in Washington D.C., which is a protest of our nation's abortion laws. There are many opinions out there about abortion, but the Truth that cannot be disputed is that all life is sacred. Why? Because God created life and made all living things. In the creation accounts recorded in Genesis chapters 1 & 2, God called His creation *"very good"* (Genesis 1:31). God's crowning creation was humankind, since we are created in His image (Genesis 1:27). Perhaps part of being made in the image of God is the ability to also "create." God created *ex nihilo*, (out of nothing), but we have the awesome privilege to create human life – the greatest gift God has given us; to abuse that gift is a huge insult to God, our Creator.

Human life is intrinsically sacred, and must always be protected, in all forms: young and old, black and white, male and female, rich and poor, educated and uneducated, sick and healthy, born and pre-born; why? Because God said so. Society tells us that some people are worth more than others, or are of greater value, depending on what they contribute, depending even on their physical appearance, health, age, or their wealth and status in society. The Bible says *"God shows no partiality"* (Romans 2:11 & Acts 10:34), and that if we show partiality, we commit sin (James 2:9).

What does God say about those who cannot defend themselves, such as the marginalized, the poor, and the unborn? Proverbs 24:11-12 says, *"If you hold back from rescuing those taken away to death, those who go staggering to the slaughter; if you say, 'Look, we did not know this-does not he who keeps watch over your soul know it? And will he not repay all according to their deeds?"* As Christ- followers, we are to defend all life as sacred, all life as made in His image, all life as a beautiful gift from God with purpose for the work that He wants to accomplish. Acts 17:25 says that God *"Himself gives to all mortals life and breath and all things,"* which truly does make all life sacred and beautiful; this is not up for debate depending on our feelings or circumstances. Truth is not relative, but it is fixed by God and is absolute according to His Word. May we not play God and make our own truths, but live obediently by His perfect Truth.

A Test of Character

Theologian and author Thomas Kempis (1380-1471) wrote, "The quality of a man's virtue is best displayed in difficult times, and far from weakening him, such times reveal him for what he really is." Only when difficult times come do we know what we are capable of, what we can endure, and how strong we really are. It is in the difficult times that we can witness the power of the Holy Spirit at work within us. When life is easy, when things are going our way, when we are happy and basically carefree, our character is not tested. The great men and women of the Bible experienced painfully difficult times in their lives, but their true character was revealed in the midst of these times, and the power of God was fully on display.

Abraham is one example. He longed for a child for many years, but his wife Sarah was barren, and they grew old together, with no children. When they finally had their son Isaac, God told Abraham to sacrifice his son, as a test. Abraham must have had great faith and a strong character, because he proceeded to do as God told him. Abraham however, must have known God would give Isaac back to him in some way, since, *"He (Abraham), said to his servants, 'Stay here with the donkey while I and the boy go over there. We will worship and then we will come back to you'"* (Genesis 22:5). Abraham did not say *"I will come back,"* but he said *"we will come back."* How would anyone know the great strength and faith of Abraham if God did not allow him to go through this trial?

Joseph was another man in the Bible who suffered greatly at the hands of his family; Genesis 37-45 tells his story. Joseph's brothers sold him into slavery to the Egyptians, told his father he died, and forgot all about him. Many years later however, after Joseph rose to prominence in Egypt, being only second in power in the entire country next to the Pharaoh, his brothers unknowingly came to him for relief from the famine in Israel. Surprisingly, Joseph helped them and never sought revenge. That quality of forgiveness and love might not have been known had Joseph not experienced such pain and hardship in his life.

Maybe you are going through a very difficult, trying, and painful time in your life; these times will reveal who you really are. Do you trust God's faithfulness to pull you through? Like Abraham, can you believe God can do the impossible? Like Joseph, perhaps someone has done you great harm and hurt you deeply; can you forgive them rather than feel hatred and seek revenge? How else can our faith grow unless we endure trials? Jesus' disciple Peter wrote, "*Herein you are triumphant, even if it is presently necessary to be saddened by trials of many sorts, this must be so you can give proof of your faith, a more precious thing than gold tested by fire, this proof will bring you praise, and glory, and honor when Jesus Christ is revealed*" (I Peter 1:6-7). Anyone can endure good times; only the strong in faith and character can endure the hard times.

Many of us in the past (and maybe even currently), are not holding up too well under pressure; this is the time to seek the Lord in humble prayer, and ask for *His* strength, which He will freely give when we open ourselves up to Him. Jesus said, "*With God all things are possible*" (Mark 10:27b). God tests the faithful among us by bringing us through fire; He said, "*I will refine them like silver and test them like gold*" (Zechariah 13:9). God promises to be faithful to His people and to give us all we need to endure the trials of life; He did so all through the Bible, and He still does today. If you are being tested and tried, remain close to Jesus, and He will surely carry you through, making you a strong and beautiful piece of gold, where your true character will be revealed.

Holiday Reflections

New Year's Day

Looking Back

One of my New Year's traditions is to look back at the past year on my calendar, transfer over birthdays and other important dates onto my new calendar, and review the year that has just ended. In looking at my calendar, I recount the celebrations I was a part of, the special times I spent with family and friends, the vacation or trips I may have taken, the conferences, work and volunteer tasks I engaged in, church meetings and events I participated in, and all of the good and perhaps sometimes not so good events that transpired in the past year. In recounting the events of the year that has just ended, I am reminded of a Scripture in Isaiah 63:7, which says, *"I will recount the gracious deeds of the Lord, the praiseworthy acts of the Lord, because of all that the Lord has done for us, and the great favor to the house of Israel that He has shown them according to His mercy, according to the abundance of His steadfast love."* I am grateful God does things for us according to His mercy, and not according to what we deserve!

Every year has a mixture of both happy and sad events: babies are born, people die, the circle of life continues. Each year brings both celebrations and challenges, but, as Christians, we know that nothing happens outside of the will and knowledge of God, whether or not we understand. For some people, a year may bring more sorrow than joy, but we must never forget as Isaiah said, the "gracious and praiseworthy deeds of the Lord" and all that our Savior does for us, "according to His mercy." It is far too easy to recount the sorrows and negative aspects of life, but we need to remember what King David wrote in Psalm 30:5, *"Weeping may linger for the night, but joy comes with the morning."* Our weeping and our sorrows do not last forever. We serve a faithful and just God who does indeed bring us His joy if we open our lives to Him.

I must also remember that in addition to looking back on the events in my own life, even more so, I need to look back on the wondrous things that God has done in and through my life and in the lives of those I know. I need to recount the majesty, the wonder, the love and the mercy of a God who intimately loves us, and to see His hand in all events and circumstances. Most of us beginning a new year look on with anticipation and hope for good things to come, but whatever will come our way this year, let us remember to look for the goodness of God in all circumstances, knowing He will indeed show us His mercy, *"according to the abundance of His steadfast love."*

Lenten Season:

Broccoli and Lent

There was a comic in our church bulletin recently of two boys walking home from school. One boy said to the other, "I made a New Year's resolution to eat broccoli. If I can't stand it, I'll give it up for Lent." I thought the comic was cute. What is Lent anyway, and why do some Christians give things up? Would there be any significance to giving up things we "can't stand," like this boy said about broccoli? I once had a friend who said he was going to give up bubble gum for Lent. I responded that I had never seen him chew bubble gum, and he just smiled.

The word Lent is not found in the Bible, but it is a spiritual discipline that some Christians follow. Lent is the period preceding Easter that in the Christian Church is devoted to fasting and repentance in commemoration of Christ's fasting in the wilderness for forty days. In the Western Church it runs from Ash Wednesday to Holy Saturday and includes forty days, minus the Sabbaths. On the Sabbath days during Lent, we can enjoy the full blessings of all God has given us, and we break the Lenten fast for that day. The purpose of Lent is to prepare a believer for Good Friday and Easter through prayer, through seeking repentance of sins, and through self-denial. This event is observed in the Anglican, Eastern Orthodox, Lutheran, Methodist, and Roman Catholic churches. Some evangelical churches also observe the Lenten season. The Lenten season culminates in the annual commemoration of Holy Week, marking the death, burial, and resurrection of Jesus, beginning on Good Friday and Jesus' crucifixion, which ultimately culminates in the joyful celebration on Easter Sunday of the Resurrection of Jesus Christ. The Lenten season is a time of reflection on our sinful nature and the cost of our sins to our Lord and Savior, who willingly suffered and died in our place to redeem us to God. Fasting or denying oneself of something one normally enjoys does not make a person holier or add to their salvation, but is merely a discipline to draw our minds towards the Passion of Christ and all He gave up for us – His very life. The Lenten season is a time of contemplation, prayer, and self-denial for the purpose of giving ourselves fully to Christ. It is a daily reminder that we have indeed *"been crucified with Christ: nevertheless I live, yet not I, but Christ lives in me,"* as the Apostle Paul wrote in Galatians 2:20. When we give up something we enjoy, or if we fast, it is just a small reminder of all Jesus gave up for us.

On Ash Wednesday some people will go to their churches and get ashes placed on their foreheads in the sign of the Cross. The ashes represent our mortality and are an outward sign of our sinfulness, transformed by the power of the Cross. Many pastors will say as they place the ash on their parishioner's foreheads, "*From dust you came, and from dust you will return*" (Genesis 3:19). When we look in the mirror on Ash Wednesday and see that black smudge in the shape of a cross on our foreheads, we should be reminded that we are still sinners in need of constant conversion. It is the Church calling us back once again to the graces of our baptism, and to amend our lives as we approach the greatest celebration in the Church — Easter. So if you do get ashes on your foreheads, do not wear them with pride, but rather wear them humbly, through the beautiful grace of our loving God.

Good Friday

The Via Dolorosa

There is a beautiful song entitled, *"The Via Dolorosa,"* which literally means "the sorrowful way," the road of Jesus' suffering, which I always listen to during Holy week. The Via Dolorosa is a street within the Old City of Jerusalem, believed to be the path that Jesus walked on the way to His crucifixion. The winding route goes from the Antonia Fortress, west, to the Church of the Holy Sepulcher, a distance of about 600 meters, and is a celebrated place of Christian pilgrimage.

That long, painful road is the road Jesus walked upon on His way to the Cross. By all practical means, it looked like things were hopeless. All of the hopes His disciples and followers had of Jesus relieving them from the Roman rule and oppression they lived under seemed to have died with Jesus. Most people did not understand His mission and purpose, especially as they hailed Him King of Jerusalem on Palm Sunday (John 12:13). Several times though, Jesus told his followers, and his enemies, including Pilate, that His Kingdom *"was not of this world"* (John 18:36). However, the freedom and deliverance Jesus spoke about for three years seemed to disappear at the Cross; they just did not understand. Life looked bleak with their Messiah dying.

Like the disciples, do we base our faith on the things we see and on what appears to be occurring? Hebrews 11:1 says, *"Now faith is the reality of things being hoped for, the proof of things not being seen."* Jesus' followers did not see the whole picture. Like the Cross, things often are not as they appear, or occur for reasons unknown to us, for God's purposes.

Sometimes, we too may simply not understand or see the whole picture.

As He was dying, Jesus said, *"My God, my God, why have You forsaken Me?"* (Mark 15:34). Jesus took on all the sin of the world and was momentarily separated from God, entering the depths of Hell in our place. On the other hand, God told us that He "will never leave or forsake" us (Hebrews 13:5). What appeared to be a horrible and cruel act (Jesus' crucifixion), was actually the greatest gift and the most hope we could possibly imagine, since His death paid the price for our sins and gives us eternal life with Him.

Scripture says, *"Let us run with perseverance the race that is set before us, looking to Jesus the pioneer and perfecter of our faith, who for the sake of the joy that was set before Him endured the cross, disregarding its shame, and has taken the seat at the right hand of the throne of God"* (Hebrews 12 1b-2). The line that intrigues and amazes me in that Hebrews passage is, "for the sake of joy… Jesus endured the cross." Joy?! Jesus knew there would be joy AFTER His suffering, but He endured more than we will ever be able to imagine because of His unbelievable love for us.

Easter

Reconciliation

Sometimes Christians strongly disagree with one another, which sometimes leads to conflicts and relational problems. Even the apostle Paul had a sharp disagreement with his friend and co-laborer for Christ Barnabas, which led to a separation in their relationship. We find the story of their falling out in the book of Acts: "*After some days Paul said to Barnabas, 'Come, let us return and visit the believers in every city where we proclaimed the Lord and see how they are doing.' Barnabas wanted to take with them John called Mark. But Paul decided not to take with them one who deserted them in Pamphylia and had not accompanied them in their work. The disagreement became so sharp that they parted company; Barnabas took Mark with him and sailed away to Cyprus. But Paul chose Silas and set out...*" (Acts 15:36-40). Has this ever happened to you; such sharp disagreements with a brother or sister in Christ that you parted ways? What eventually happened with that relationship? Does it matter? As Christ-followers, it matters greatly, especially to God.

Reconciliation requires the humbling forgiveness of people on all sides of a conflict. Fortunately, Scripture tells us that Paul, Mark, and Barnabas did indeed reconcile and worked together later on (Colossians 4:10 & 2 Timothy 4:11). Paul could have remained angry with Mark for "abandoning" him. Mark could have remained angry with Paul for not wanting to take him along when they went to visit the believers in the various cities. Barnabas could have remained angry with Paul for not wanting to take his cousin Mark on that trip spoken about in Acts, but as brothers in Christ, they appeared to have forgiven one another and reconciled. When Jesus told us to forgive others, such as in the Lord's Prayer in Matthew 6:9-13, and in and the following verses, Matthew 6:14-15 (as well as many other places in the Bible), He did not say that forgiveness is contingent on how we felt. The writer to the Hebrews wrote, *"Pursue peace with everyone, and the holiness without which no one will see the Lord"* (Hebrews 12:14). Our actions should reflect the Lord's love for all of us, and our love for one another. What kind of Christian witness will we have if we do not pursue love and reconciliation with people? As followers of Christ, our goal is to glorify God and enjoy Him forever, and to bring others into the fold of His love, mercy, and forgiveness. Our words and our actions should always pursue reconciliation, love, and forgiveness, just as Christ reconciled us sinners to God the Father, through His perfect love and forgiveness towards us.

Imagine if God were like most of us: If He held grudges, if He sought revenge, and if He refused to forgive; we would surely all be lost and in big trouble! But because He loves us far more than humans are capable of loving, God desired reconciliation with His creation to the point of dying on a Cross for us, taking our sins upon Himself, and forgiving even the worst of sinners. Through His resurrection, He conquered sin and death, and gave us the chance for eternal life with Him forever. Reconciliation is what we really celebrate at Easter, by a God who is more powerful, more forgiving, and more loving than anything in the entire universe. As we celebrate Easter Sunday, let us look on the Cross, the pain, and the horror Jesus willingly experienced, in order to reconcile us to Him forever, but more importantly, to His resurrection as He completely conquered sin and death forever.

Mother's Day

A Mothers Love

Jesus performed many miracles, but probably none were as spectacular as raising someone from the dead. Most of us know about the raising of Lazarus in John 10, but Jesus actually raised someone else from the dead prior to Lazarus, which we do not hear about as often. In Luke 7:11-17, we read of Jesus' first miracle of raising someone from the dead, and it involved the grief of a mother, who was also widowed, who lived in a town called Nain.

Nain was a small village in Galilee, about 5 miles southeast of Nazareth. Nain means "pleasant" or "green pastures" and is mentioned specifically only once in the Bible, where it records the first miracle of Jesus Christ raising the dead. The boy who died was a widow's only son. While he was being carried to his grave, probably in an open coffin which was the Jewish custom, Jesus approached the large crowd in this funeral procession and told the woman, "*'Weep not'. And He touched the coffin: and the pallbearers stood still. And He said, 'Young man, I say to you, Arise.' And the corpse sat up and began talking, and Jesus delivered him to his mother.*" (Luke 7:13-15). Jesus risked ritual uncleanness by touching this young man's coffin (Numbers 20:16), though He often did things that would have made Him "unclean" when He performed miracles, such as healing the sick and the lepers. Jesus lovingly reached out and touched the "unclean" people because they were in need of His healing touch. We too must make ourselves vulnerable, reaching out to the "unclean" when they need the love of Jesus and to feel the power of His love, through us.

Jesus appeared to have had a special place in His heart for mothers. Jesus raised from the dead the widow of Nain's son, who would have been her only help and possible source of income, and had compassion on her. In biblical times, women generally did not work outside of their homes, but took care of their homes and families full time. Women relied on their husband's for support, or if they had died, on their oldest son to provide for them. Without her only son, this widow was without hope and may have had to beg in order to survive. But then came Jesus. Only in Jesus do we have hope. Jesus had a strong love for His own mother Mary, and made sure there was someone to care for her after His death, as she too was probably widowed (since we read no more of Joseph, and who was not present at Jesus' death), and told His disciple John to care for her (John 19: 26&27).

One of the Ten Commandments, and the only one with a promise, is to *"Honor your father and your mother, so that you may live long in the land the Lord your God is giving you"* (Exodus 20:12). Whether we have a good relationship with our mothers or not, we are to honor them, as the person who gave us life. Some of us no longer have our mothers here on earth, but we can remember them as gifts from God, and honor mothers everywhere this weekend. We need to be aware of the outcast moms, who others may see as "unclean," and also extend to them the special love and care Jesus had not only for His own mother Mary and for the widow of Nain, but for all mothers. We can also share with all people, as was true for the widow of Nain, that it is only through Jesus that we find real hope.

Memorial Day

Memorial Day and the Sabbath

At the end of May, we will celebrate Memorial Day. Memorial Day is a federal holiday in the United States set aside to remember the people who died while serving in our country's armed forces. The holiday, which is currently observed every year on the last Monday of May, originated as Decoration Day after the American Civil War in 1868, when the Grand Army of the Republic, an organization of Union veterans founded in Decatur, Illinois, established it as a time for the nation to decorate the graves of the Union war dead with flowers. By the 20th century, there were competing Union and Confederate holiday traditions which were celebrated on different days. Eventually they merged, and Memorial Day extended to honor all Americans who died while serving in the military. This holiday marks the start of the unofficial summer vacation season, which is probably what most of us think about, rather than its intended purpose.

I liken Memorial Day to Sunday's – our Sabbath. Many people basically view Sundays as a day to sleep in, to golf, to fish, to kayak, and to engage in favorite hobbies. While enjoying hobbies can be a good thing, we should also remember what our Sabbath was intended for – primarily worship. When God created the world, Scripture says, *"Thus the heavens and the earth were finished, and all their multitude. And on the seventh day God finished the work that He had done, and He rested on the seventh day from all the work that He had done. So God blessed the seventh day and made it holy, because on it God rested from all the work that He had done in creation"* (Genesis

2:1-3). Now we realize of course that God did not really need to rest – after all, He is God! God never tires like we do, but He created a day to "rest" as an example to us – a day to rest from our daily chores and work, and to gather together with fellow believers and worship. God joyfully made the Sabbath for us. In addition to going to the synagogue to worship, Jesus healed on the Sabbath and did many good things, which angered the Pharisees. Jesus said, *"The Sabbath was made to serve mankind, and not mankind for the Sabbath"* (Mark 2:27) when He was speaking to the Pharisees, who made their own very strict rules as to how to observe the Sabbath, that went beyond the parameters of God.

Hopefully at some point this Memorial weekend, we will remember those who laid down their lives for our freedoms in this country, in addition to its being the start of summer and the fun activities and vacations we may have planned. But let us also remember the One who laid down His life for our freedom from sin and death – Jesus Christ, our Lord and Savior. While we do need to gather with others on Sundays to worship, our lives should be lived each day in worship and service to our Lord and Master, Jesus Christ, who died not just for the people in our country, but for all people, from all times, throughout the world, for our ultimate freedom – freedom in Christ, which no man can take away

Father's Day

A Father's Love

Most of us know the parable of the prodigal son in Luke 15:11-32. Our focus is often on the son, and sometimes on his older brother, but with Father's Day this weekend, I am going to focus on the father in this story. When Jesus told this parable, the father figure represents Jesus' own Father – God. There are several components to this story that speak of the wonderful characteristics of the father, who again, represents our Heavenly Father.

To begin, the younger son actually asked his father for his share of the inheritance while his father was still alive, which was an insult. Asking for his inheritance early is almost like saying he wished his father was already dead, and his interest lied more in what his dad could give to him than in the man himself. The father, without complaint or hesitation, gave the share to his sons. The first characteristic we see of this father is that he was approachable. Even though the younger son asked for something that most people would feel was inappropriate and greedy, the father still gave the son what he wanted. Just a few days later, the younger son left home with his new wealth that his father gave him, which probably hurt his dad's feelings. The second characteristic we see in this father is that he was generous. He was free to say no to his son when he asked for the inheritance, but he did not; he freely gave.

After the prodigal son squandered all of his money on wild and dissolute living, he wanted to come back home to his father, since at least he would have a place to live and food to eat, which he no longer had. Luke 15:20 says, *"So he set off and went to his father. But while he was still far off, his father saw him and was filled with compassion; he ran and put his arms around him and kissed him."* We see several more beautiful characteristics of the father in this verse. First, we notice that the father was looking and waiting for his son's return; he did not forget about him, but patiently waited for him to return to his senses and come back home. We then see the love and compassion of the father, rather than anger, resentment and disappointment.

The father was not considering his own hurt feelings, but only the well-being of his son who he still loved very much. Also, in those days, only slaves and messengers would run. For the father to run to his son, especially a wealthy man as he must have been, that would have been degrading, which showed his humility, and selflessness. After the prodigal son admitted his sins and spoke of his unworthiness to even be called a son, the father joyfully called for his slaves to, *"Put the best robe on him and put a ring on his hand, and sandals on his feet"* (Luke 15:22). The robe represented a festal garment that would not be worn while working, the ring was a symbol of authority, and slaves did not wear shoes. The father was taking his son back with no questions asked. Most fathers would be angry upon seeing their son, ask many questions, call him to give an account of what he did with the money, and probably make him work off his debt. The father in this story did none of those things; he merely forgave. The father then said, *"And kill the calf we are fattening: and let us eat and be merry. For this my son I thought was dead and is alive; he was lost but is found!"* (Verses 23 & 24). The father expressed joy in the return of his son, as God accepts those of us who have rebelled and sinned against him, but return in humility – even if our motives are selfish as was the prodigal's.

We serve a wonderfully approachable, generous, patient, giving, compassionate, forgiving and loving God who delights in our return to Him and always takes us back. Some of us no longer have fathers on earth, some of us have fathers who do not have these characteristics, and some of us have wonderful fathers. I was fortunate to have a wonderful father, though he is now in Heaven, and I miss him every day. I also know that I have an awesome heavenly Father who loves us more than any human being can love, who is relentlessly pursuing us, watching for our return when we stray, and lovingly accepting us as we are, forgiving us, and making us His children. What a great God we serve!

4th of July

Freedom

In America, we celebrate our many freedoms and even have a federal holiday commemorating the adoption of the Declaration of Independence on July 4, 1776. The Continental Congress declared that the thirteen American colonies regarded themselves as a new nation, the United States of America, and were no longer part of the British Empire. We celebrate our freedom as a nation, and a nation that has more freedoms than many other nations in the world. One wonderful freedom we enjoy is the freedom of religion and worship. We do not have underground churches as many countries are forced to have where Christianity is illegal. We can pray in public and read our Bibles without fear of imprisonment or persecution, which some people experience in other parts of the world; these freedoms should never be taken for granted.

As Christians, we also celebrate a truly remarkable freedom – freedom in Christ. Jesus told us that, "*If you continue in My Word, then you are without a doubt My disciples; and you will know the truth, and the truth will make you free*" (John 8:31-32). Free from what? From the law of sin and death (Romans 8:2), which cannot give life. Only Jesus can give us life; but as He said, IF we continue in His Word. Paul wrote in his letter to the Galatians, "*Now the Lord is the Spirit, and where the Spirit of the Lord is, there is freedom*" (Galatians 3:17). So what are we to do with this freedom that Christ has given to us? Paul also wrote, "*But now that you have been freed from sin and enslaved to God, the advantage you get is sanctification*" (Romans 6:22). When we break the yoke and bondage of sin, we are then free to allow the Holy Spirit to work in us, to sanctify us, and to make us more like Jesus every day. We are now a new creation, created to do good works (Ephesians 2:10).

   We are also free to make good choices. Choices guided by the power and wisdom of the Holy Spirit, rather than by our own sinful natures. If we truly love God, we will make choices that bring Him honor and glory, and that reflect His nature. We will also make choices that lift up other people and are made humbly, looking out for the interests of others over ourselves (Philippians 2:3). The freedom Christ gives to us allows us to make choices that bring us, and others joy, as we live to show the love of Jesus each day, to everyone we encounter. Jesus can break the chains of sin, of any kind: addictions, bitterness, hatred, unforgiveness, or anything that keeps us living the life God intends for us to live. Jesus wants us to be free and not tied down to a yoke of sin. The apostle Paul wrote that we have, "*been set free from sin*" (Romans 6:18) and can live in the fullness of Jesus Christ, who has set us free. Galatians 5:1 says, "*For freedom Christ has set us free. Stand firm, therefore, and do not submit again to a yoke of slavery.*" Through Jesus Christ, we can live lives of true freedom, of which we cannot find anywhere else. There are many freedoms that we experience as Americans, but I hope we also consider the bountiful freedoms we have in Christ, who broke our chains from the slavery sin puts us in, and find life – abundant, joyful life, as new creations, sanctified through the Holy Spirit, to live as God intended for us to live.

Labor Day

Labor

When man and woman were first created, they worked. In the creation account as recorded in Genesis, it says, "*The Lord God took the man and put him in the Garden of Eden to work it and keep it*" (Genesis 2:15). It was not until after the Fall, when Adam and Eve sinned, that work became difficult. God said to Adam, "*Because you have listened to the voice of your wife and have eaten of the tree of which I commanded you, 'You shall not eat of it,' cursed is the ground because of you; in pain you shall eat of it all the days of your life; thorns and thistles it shall bring forth for you: and you shall eat the plants of the field. By the sweat of your face you shall eat bread, till you return to the ground*" (Genesis 3:17-19a).

Even though humankind has sinned, God still lovingly gives us some rest from our work. God actually commands us to rest. In Exodus 20, God gave Moses the Ten Commandments, and the fourth commandment God said, "*Remember the Sabbath day, to keep it holy. Six days you shall labor, and do all your work, but the seventh day is a Sabbath to the Lord your God. On it you shall not do any work, you, or your son, or your daughter, your male servant, or your female servant, or your livestock, or the sojourner who is within your gates. For in six days the Lord made heaven and earth, the sea, and all that is in them, and rested on the seventh day. Therefore the Lord blessed the Sabbath day and made it holy*" Exodus 20:8-11).

There are of course exceptions where people must work on the Sabbath, such as medical workers, police and fire workers, priests and pastors, etc., but all of these professions still (usually) get at least a day or two off on other days of the week to rest, and hopefully to worship. God, in His infinite mercy, gave us the Sabbath as a gift. Jesus said, *"The Sabbath was made for man, not man for the Sabbath"* (Mark 2:27). The gospels record Jesus doing many good deeds on the Sabbath, including healing the sick, which the Pharisees considered work. When they criticized Jesus for His "works" of mercy, it always amazed me that they were not surprised that Jesus was even able to perform these miracles of healing, but rather, they criticized Him for them, such as we find in Mark chapters 2 and 3.

Work, whether we like our job or not, is still a blessing since it is the means that we have to provide for ourselves, our families, and to help others. In his letter to the Ephesians, the apostle Paul wrote, *"Let the thief no longer steal, but rather let him labor, doing honest work with his own hands, so that he may have something to share with anyone in need"* (Ephesians 4:28). We are not to work merely for ourselves, but to share with others, to tithe and give to the work of the Gospel, and to live generous lives, which in itself, is a wonderful blessing. This week as you drive to work, reflect on the many blessings God has given you through your work, and how you can be a blessing to others as you labor, all in the name of Christ.

Halloween

Reform Halloween

Many of us take our children or grandchildren out for Halloween. Some Christians do not like the "gory" aspects of Halloween, and wish to celebrate something else instead. Here is an idea: what about celebrating Reformation Day? What is Reformation Day you ask? October 31 is Reformation Day. What exactly is it, and what does that have to do with us? A lot. On October 31, 1517, the Augustinian monk Martin Luther nailed his 95 theses (questions) and propositions for debate to a church door in Wittenberg, Germany. Luther's main issue was that the Roman Catholic Church (which was the only Christian church at that time) taught salvation through faith and works; but how are we really saved? Is that correct? No. We are saved by grace alone – God's infinite and loving grace. Somewhere along the line, the Church lost the focus of Jesus and replaced the focus on humankind.

The apostle Paul encountered that same incorrect thinking in the years around A.D. 50-55 when he first started his missionary journeys. Paul wrote to the Church in Ephesus, *"For through faith and His loving kindness are you rescued; it is not of your own doing; it was not your action, but God's gift that saved you: not personal action, lest any man should boast"* (Ephesians 2:8-9). There is nothing we can do to save ourselves. We need Jesus.

In the 1500's, people were paying Indulgences to the Church for the forgiveness of sins. Luther saw the corruption of the Church and the ignorance of a mostly illiterate society who did not know what the Bible taught and who were fearful of not going to Heaven. Luther made a stand. For three days the Catholic Church asked Luther to withdraw his questions and complaints, but he did not. Martin Luther did not intend to start a whole new church (the Protestant Church), but because he refused to back down on his correct reading of the Bible concerning salvation, he broke away from the Catholic Church, and thus began the Protestant Reformation.

Fortunately, over the years there has been a lot of reform in the Catholic Church and some of their teachings (such as Indulgences) were stopped. A proper reading of Scripture is now possible, with a focus on Jesus, and the availability of the Bible to the average person to read for themselves may not have occurred had it not been for Martin Luther and the Reformation; that truly is something to celebrate! 2017 marked the 500th anniversary of the Reformation, and many churches had huge celebrations. This change in focus off of ourselves, and on to Jesus, is the direct result of the Reformation. As Christ followers, the Holy Spirit places a desire in us to obey God's commands, to love Him and our neighbors, and to live better, holy, sanctified lives as a result of our salvation, not as a means to our salvation.

As Christians, we must always keep our focus on Jesus, and never on ourselves. We are saved through our faith in Jesus, which is a gift in itself from God. No matter how much good we think we do, it will never get us into Heaven, "*since all have sinned and fall short of the glory of God*" (Romans 3:23), but the good news is that "*being justified by free grace through the ransom paid in Christ Jesus: whom God set forth to make atonement through faith in His blood*" (Romans 3:24-25a). Let us all pray for great faith, and remember to always keep our focus where it needs to be – not on ourselves, but on Jesus.

Veteran's Day

Forgiveness and 9-11

Our country will hopefully always commemorate the anniversary of the terrorist attacks on September 11, in honor of those who died, in honor of our first responders, and in honor of our veterans who fight for our freedoms. There is a famous misquote, that I have even used, which says, "Those who ignore history are doomed to repeat it." The actual quote was written by philosopher George Santayana (1863-1952) in his book "Reason in Common Sense; The Life of Reason Volume 1, which says, "Those who cannot remember the past are condemned to repeat it." Monday, I read various articles about the remembrance of 9-11, and came across several quotes from families who lost loved ones on that terrible day. One man who lost his brother said, "We will never forget, and we will never forgive."

We all know of the infamous flight 93 on 9-11 which was headed for the Capitol building. The passengers on that plane decided to take over and prevent this flight from crashing into another building as they spoke to family members by phone and learned of the terrorist/suicide plane crashes into the World Trade Center towers. Flight 93 crashed the plane into a field in Somerset County Pennsylvania, just 12 minutes from the Capitol, and miraculously, no one on the ground was killed; perhaps thousands of other people were saved when that plane never made it to the Capitol building. We all remember Todd Beamer who, along with several other men on flight 93, said, "Let's roll," as they pushed a food and beverage cart towards the cockpit, trying to overtake the Al-Qaeda terrorists. Seven crew members and 33 passengers died in that crash. There was a ceremony at that spot in Pennsylvania Monday, where 40 tubular chimes were placed, in honor of each of the lives lost in that crash. Those chimes will continuously sound as the wind blows through them on that mountain top memorial. In contrast to the previous man's statement concerning the loss of his brother, a woman, who lost her daughter on that flight spoke about the ceremony and said, "The bells, the ringing, I could hear our daughter's voice in it. She loved to sing. She loved to praise the Lord." Wow! Instead of being filled with hatred, anger and revenge, this mother sought the comfort of God, knowing how her daughter loved the Lord and sang His praise. While this woman surely experienced incredible grief, sadness, and yes, even anger at her daughter's death, this mother did not speak of those emotions. Perhaps she too loves the Lord, who alone can bring her comfort and the *"peace that passes understanding"* (Philippians 4:7).

I did not have any friends or family members die on 9-11, so I cannot imagine the many emotions that must accompany those who did. The question I put on the board for this week in the lunch room, is, does God require that we forgive something even as heinous and evil as the 9-11 terrorist attacks? The answer of course, is yes. Easier said than done, I know, and even easier for those of us who did not know anyone personally. However, as Jesus was literally being nailed to the Cross, He said, *"Father forgive them, for they do not understand what they are doing"* (Luke 23:34). This week, may we never forget the past, so that we may learn and grow from it, but may we also never forget the incredible love of our Savior, who in the midst of His anguish, cried to His, and to our Father, to forgive, for the many who do not know what they do.

Thanksgiving

Thankful For Prison?

One of the clients I was talking to at the Mission last week was thankful for what seemed a strange thing; he was thankful he went to prison. I have heard several people tell me this, which at first sounds surprising, but makes sense once their story is told. The man who was talking to me told me his life was heading along a path of destruction, and had incarceration not stopped him, he would have probably died in a hopeless and lost state. Jail gave him time to contemplate his life and his death; it was the place where he found a Bible, which he had not read before, and with plenty of time now on his hands, he began to read. This man's story is a common story – of finding Jesus Christ in jail, and for the first time, experiencing true love, joy, forgiveness, and freedom. We often go through various trials, circumstances and difficulties in life where we can later look back and be thankful. The Bible says, "*in everything give thanks: for this is the desire of God in Christ Jesus concerning you*" (I Thessalonians 5:18). What is most challenging though is not being thankful in retrospect, but being thankful in the moment – in the difficult and painful moments, even in jail.

I think of the story of Joseph in the book of Genesis where he was sold into slavery by his brothers who were jealous of him. He was taken to Egypt as a slave, then thrown in jail on a false accusation, but later became a very powerful man, second only to Pharaoh in all of Egypt. Joseph then saved his family and many others from famine when he ruled that country. Many extremely difficult times in our lives, such as prison for my client, slavery and imprisonment for Joseph, or other circumstances in our own lives, are not easy for us to be thankful, but we must realize, *"That in all things God works for the good of those who love Him, who have been called according to His purpose"* (Romans 8:28). During this Thanksgiving season, can we truly be thankful for all things?

Most of us will sit around a table with friends and family, with far too much food, in comfortable homes, and of course, have many things of which we can be thankful. But we know there are many people who are not in such privileged positions; maybe some of you reading this right now are not. Perhaps a reader may be alone, may be lonely, may have just lost a loved one, or maybe even be incarcerated. So let us remember those whose life may be difficult right now. Let us remember those in prison, and pray that they take their time now to contemplate God and His forgiveness, like my client, and experience God's mercy and love. Let us keep those in prayer who are suffering from illness or loneliness, and let us always look for opportunities to help, to love, and to serve those whom God puts in our paths, and be the hands and feet of Jesus in a world that needs Him so very much.

Advent Season

Twelve Days of Christmas

The Christmas season is filled with so much beautiful music, especially the classic Christmas carols such as my favorite, O Holy Night. Many of you may know the song, "The Twelve Days of Christmas," which has some unusual lyrics, but which has an interesting history. Legend has it that someone wrote this carol back in the 1500's as a catechism for young Catholic Christians, with each numbered phrase designed to help them remember the Faith without giving away the Catholic identity of the singer.

The partridge in a pear tree was Jesus Christ. The two turtle doves were the Old and New Testaments, and the three French hens stood for faith, hope and love. Four calling birds were the gospels of Matthew, Mark, Luke and John. The five golden rings represented the Torah or Law, the first five books of the Old Testament. Six geese–a–laying stood for the six days of creation, and the seven swans a swimming were the seven-fold gifts of the Holy Spirit. Eight maids-a-milking were the eight Beatitudes as found in Matthew chapter 5, and nine ladies dancing were the fruits of the Holy Spirit, found in Galatians chapter 5 (love, joy, peace, patience, kindness, generosity, faithfulness, gentleness and self-control). The ten-lords-a-leaping were the Ten Commandments. Eleven pipers piping stood for the eleven faithful disciples and the twelve drummers drumming symbolized the twelve doctrinal points in the Apostles Creed.

I remember as a child singing that song and having fun with it, unaware of any theological meaning or significance.

I am not sure if the legend about its underlying meaning is true or not, but it is good to know that even what sounds like a secular Christmas song is actually about the Christian faith. We all hear the phrase, "Let's keep Christ in Christmas," yet it is so true. While we can indeed have fun decorating our homes, baking special Christmas goodies, and buying Christmas gifts for one another, may we remember during this hectic time of year, that Jesus truly is the reason for the season.

Christmas

The First Hectic Christmas

Shopping, wrapping, malls, baking, cooking, decorating, Christmas dinners, music programs, plays, cards to address and mail…yes, this time of year can be quite loud and hectic. Try as I may, I do sometimes lose focus of the Incarnation – God in the flesh – Jesus, whose birth we celebrate. I do enjoy though, the traditions we have embraced as a culture in our celebration of Christmas, especially all of the lights, which I hang throughout my house, both inside and outside.

The lights remind me that in a dark and sinful world, Jesus came to bring us the light of the Good News. An unusually bright star led the wise men and shepherds to Jesus. When I get frustrated at that string of lights which has just burnt out, may I remember the Light of the world – Jesus the Christ.

I love shopping for a live Christmas tree that makes my home smell of pine. The lights on the tree twinkle in the dark, as Jesus hopefully shines in our lives. The tree also reminds me that our Savior hung on a tree thirty three years after His birth, to make a way for us to be reconciled to God and to live forever with Him in eternity.

The gifts under my tree remind me of the kingly gifts the wise men brought to the Christ child, of whom they knew was a King, and gladly shared in their homage to this new born King. The gifts and the cards which I send out and receive cause me to pause in thanksgiving at the wonderful friends and family God has blessed me with, and the joy and fulfillment they bring to my life.

And the food, yes, the way- too- much- food and goodies that we eat at this time of year, makes me ever so grateful that God truly does provide, much more than we really need, and of our need to share with others from our bounty.

In the gospel of Luke, chapter 2, we read the Christmas story. When we see movies or watch plays, and when we think of the lowly manger and humble birth place of Jesus, we usually do not think of all the noise, fear, and excitement of that time. However, while the shepherds were simply out watching their flocks, as they did every other night, out of nowhere, an angel appeared, frightening them, who said, "*Stop being afraid: for behold, I announce good news and great joy for all people*" (Luke 2:10). Most of us would probably be rather frightened if an angel appeared and started speaking to us! While the angel was still talking to the shepherds, "*And suddenly there appeared the armies of heaven saying, 'Glory to God on high and peace on earth peace to men of good will'*" (Luke 2:13-14). What beautiful noise must have been occurring with the angel's proclamation! When the angels left, the shepherds "*hurried off*" (Luke 2:16) to find Jesus. There was noise, fear, excitement, and rushing around as was evident according to Luke 2. While we are hurrying around this season, may we remember the shepherds who also "hurried off," though they left in haste to find this King. May we also keep King Jesus in our minds and hearts as we too hurry around to get our holiday preparations complete.

My favorite verse in the Christmas story is Luke 2:19, which says, "*But Mary treasured up all these things and pondered them in her heart.*" After all the rushing around, the noise of the shopping malls, and even the "fear" of not having everything ready on time is done, let us take a moment and ponder what this holiday means to us, and like Mary, treasure it in our hearts. Merry Christmas everyone!

New Year's Eve

A New Start

It's that time again when people make New Year's resolutions, which often are not kept, or only for a short time. Gym membership's increase in January, but taper off as the year progresses. We have so many good intentions, but we often fall short in keeping them and carrying through on those intentions. Our spiritual intentions and resolutions though, are more important than our physical ones. We may want to eat less, exercise more, quit smoking, etc., which are all good goals, but what about the more important disciplines, such as spending more time in the Word of God, in prayer, in worship, and drawing closer to Jesus each day? Some people begin a reading plan to go through the Bible in a year (which only requires reading three chapters a day!) and start out well in January, but like exercise, taper off and find at the end of the year the Bible has not been completed or even read very much. God knows our frailties and short- comings, and the apostle Paul wrote that we all sin and have all fallen short of God's will and intentions for us (Romans 3:23). Thankfully, even though we do fall short, we are justified by God's grace, through faith in Christ Jesus.

We may feel like we have failed when we do not keep a resolution, but I am so thankful that God allows us a fresh start, especially when we may feel like we have failed Him. God continuously forgives us, and like the father of the Prodigal son in the Gospel of Luke chapter 15, He waits for us to return to Him so that He can strengthen us and give us another chance – another year so to speak, to live for Him. We can never fall too far from the arms of God's grace. Romans chapter 3 goes on to say that we can only live righteously through the power of the Holy Spirit who gives us faith, so we have no place to boast. Paul wrote, "*that a man is given right standing with God on the basis of faith without observance of the law*" (Romans 3:28). If we do manage to keep any of our New Year's resolutions, especially our spiritual resolutions, it is only because God gives us the strength and the power to do so, and not by anything we do on our own. We owe God everything!

Unlike people who often fail at keeping resolutions and promises, God keeps ALL of His promises to us, and the "*steadfast love of the Lord never ceases, his mercies are new every morning*" (Lamentations 3:22-23). Not only has each New Year, but each day, God faithfully kept His promises to us: promises of His love, His mercy, His forgiveness, His power, and His abiding presence in our lives. God made an eternal resolution with His people that He will be our God, that He will love us with a steadfast love, that He will never leave or forsake us, and He continuously keeps His resolution year after year into eternity. This year, if you do make any resolutions, remember God's mighty and eternal resolutions to love us, to forgive us, and to be our heavenly Father; there is no resolution greater than that!

Afterword

I am happy you have chosen to read this short book of reflections. As I wrote it, my prayer was that the reader would not settle for a short devotion each week, with Scripture verses inserted into my thoughts, but that you take some time every day, to read the words that bring healing, hope and life, which are found in the Word of God – the Holy Bible. If we stake our entire lives and eternity on our Christian faith, we must certainly know what that Faith teaches. Sunday morning sermons are great. Wednesday evening Bible studies are also helpful, but the only real way to know God (who He is, His very nature, what He expects of us, and how He displays His love and power), is found in the pages of the Bible. When we find ourselves in situations where we need to make decisions and are unsure of what to do, we will find our answers within the pages of our Bible. 2 Timothy 3:16 , *"All Scripture is inspired by God and is useful for teaching, for reproof, for correction, and for training in righteousness, so that everyone who belongs to God may be proficient, equipped for every good work."* We have all that we need for life in God's Word.

God longs for us to learn about Him, to draw close to Him, and to be in constant communion with Him, living in His presence each moment of our lives. God desires to equip us with what we need to be proficient in whatever He calls us to do, and to live out the good works that He desires. We must learn and study His Word that He has provided for us, and not let our Bibles sit and look nice on our book shelves. Thank you for taking your time to read these devotions, and may they inspire you to press in closer to our Lord and Savior Jesus Christ, each day, as He longs to fill us with the joy, the peace, and the wisdom of His Word.

Sources and References

Augustine, *City of God*, Penguin Classics Publishing, 2004

Baird, Forrest E., and Walter Kaufmann, *Ancient Philosophy second edition*, Prentice- Hall, Inc.: New Jersey, 1997.

Brother Lawrence, *The Practice of the Presence of God*. Whitaker House: New Kensington, PA, 1982.

Capra, Frank, *It's a Wonderful Life*, 1946.

Carr, Nicholas, *Utopia is Creepy*. W.W. Norton & Company: New York, 2016.

Eisley, Loren, "The Star Thrower," found in "*The Unexpected Universe*, Harcourt, Brace and World, 1969.

Green, Hollis L. (translator) *The Evergreen Devotional New Testament* (EDNT). Complete Edition, Post-Gutenberg Books: Global Ed Advance Press: Nashville, TN. 2015.

The Gideon, "*A Voice and a Vision; The Testimony of Jimmy Fortune*," June/July 2017, (p.19).

Hall, Ron and Denver Moore, with Lynn Vincent, *Same Kind of Different as Me*. W. Publishing, an imprint of Thomas Nelson: Nashville, TN, 2006.

Kempis, Thomas a', *The Imitation of Christ*. Vintage Spiritual Classics: New York, 1998.

The Legend of the Phoenix – Ancient Greek Mythology

Metzger, Bruce M. and Murphy, Roland E. (editors), *The New Oxford Annotated Bible New Revised Version*, Oxford University Press: New York, 1994.

Patti, Sandi, *The Via Doloroso*.

Piper, John, *Don't Waste Your Life*. Crossway Publishers: Wheaton, IL., 2009.

Ripken, Nik, *The Insanity of God: A True Story of Faith Resurrected,* 2013.

Stueve, Rev. Steve. *Lutheran Braille Workers Newsletter,* winter, 2016.

Studd, Charles Thompson, Goodreads Quotes from the Internet

Thompson, Hunter S., *The Proud Highway: Saga of a Desperate Southern Gentleman,* 1955-1967, The Random House Publishing Group, 1997.

About the Author

Donna (Kasik) Junker is a native of the Chicago suburbs. While attending college (where she received an under graduate degree in Philosophy) and seminary at night for many years, she owned her own business in the construction trades. After receiving the Master of Divinity, she moved to Kentucky, then several different states as she completed her Clinical Pastoral Education.

Donna worked as a hospice Chaplain for a decade. Her current position is Chaplain/Pastoral Care Coordinator with the Lexington Rescue Mission in Lexington, Kentucky. She is ordained through the World Council of Independent Christian Churches (WCICC). Her passion is cultural studies and mission work. She taught short-term intensives at a seminary in Kenya, East Africa, for 6 years, ministered at Mother Teresa's home for the dying in Calcutta, India, and worked at an AIDS hospice in Zambia, Southern Africa. Chaplain Junker has certification in Thanatology (Death, dying and bereavement counseling) and she is finishing up certification in Christian drug and alcohol counseling, which helps with her work at the Rescue Mission.

Donna is married to Dr. Paul Junker. She loves to travel, read, write, cook, run, the Arts, and all outdoor activities. She served in the Ministerial Association, and is active in her community and local church. Donna has one son, of whom she is very proud, and a wonderful daughter-in-law. She is a doting grandmother to a delightful little girl and a great step-grandson. Her greatest joy in life is being a follower of Jesus Christ, who brings peace that passes understanding, along with joy and contentment that the world could never give.

"The Lexington Rescue Mission in Lexington, Kentucky is
a wonderful place that provides spiritual care and serves
hot and nutritious meals to the poor and homeless in the
community. Also, the Mission provides clothing, blankets,
sleeping bags, toiletries, emergency utility and rent assistance, bus
passes, transitional housing for those released from prison and/
or recovering from addictions, job training, life skills, and re-entry
programs for those coming out of prison. Those interested in the
Lexington Rescue Mission, may go to www.LexingtonRescue.
org and learn about the Mission, their history, financials, staff,
Statement of Faith, social services, volunteer opportunities,
special events, how to contact or donate to the Mission, or to
follow their Blog."

Books by the Author

*Three Weeks in Africa
ISBN: 978-1-935434-13-9

"We as the American hospices are not sent to help the poor African hospices, but to deepen relationships with them, to assess needs and to discover how they function. We can share our knowledge with them, and they in turn can share their knowledge and insight with us." Hospice and Palliative Care is a new concept in Africa, and is established, funded and carried out in different ways than American hospices. The author's 3-pronged purpose in writing this book is to: 1) Approach hospice care from a missional point of view, 2) Share the importance of compassionate, faith-based end-of-life care, and 3) Understand and appreciate Zambia's challenges of hospice and palliative care.

*Kenya: A Priority on My Bucket List
ISBN: 978-1-935434-63-4

A list of things to do or accomplish before exiting this life is called a bucket list. One of the items on the author's bucket list was to go somewhere in Africa to see the wild animals in their natural habitat. Little did she know that Kenya, East Africa would become like a second home and would offer far more than a safari ride. Traveling to Kenya seven times, the author gives a detailed account of her experiences and brings to light the clash of cultures which can cause misunderstandings between missionaries and Kenyans. The cross-cultural lessons learned in this book can be applied to missions anywhere.

Recovery: A Return to the Self
ISBN: 978-1-935434-51-1

Using real-life situations, the author demonstrates principles and practices to recover the true self lost along the way. The blueprint the author used in her own recovery is like a roadmap to protect and guide - not just a rule book. As a hospice chaplain, the author witnessed first-hand the wisdom of the dying, but it was after working with the poor and dying in India that she created the spiritual 12-step program outlined in this book.

Thinking Outside the Box ...About Love
ISBN: 978-1-935434-00-5

It begins with seeking and ends with discovery; it is a deeply personal story of warm hopes and cold realities. It is a journey of conviction, compelling both the writer and the reader to look at the world differently and start, Thinking Outside the Box.. About Love. This book tells of Donna in the role of VA Chaplain who demonstrates true, Christian love for the lost and suffering.

First Day Devotions
ISBN 978-1-935434-87-0

In my work as a Chaplain/Pastoral Care Coordinator at the Lexington Rescue Mission in Lexington, Kentucky, part of my job is to write a weekly devotional for the staff. Each Wednesday afternoon I sit in my office, pray, and write my devotion, then email it to all of the staff. Each week several of the Mission staff sends me wonderfully kind and uplifting feedback from my devotions, which I do not deserve, but give glory to God if the devotionals have touched hearts and minds. After doing this part of my job for a couple of months, I decided to compile these devotions into a small book that could be used not only for the staff, but also for clients, and perhaps in homes and churches. I have included many of the devotions written at the Mission in this book and pray God uses them to uplift you.

Meditations: A Collection of Weekly & Holiday Reflections
ISBN 978-1-434535-94-8

As I wrote this book, my prayer was that the reader would not settle for a short devotion each week, with Scripture verses inserted into my thoughts, but that they would take some time every day, to read the words that bring healing, hope and life, which are found in the Word of God – the Holy Bible. If we stake our entire lives and eternity on our Christian faith, we must certainly know what that Faith teaches.

*The first four books were published under the author's maiden name: Donna Kasik.

These books may be ordered at
www.gea-books.com/bookstore or
from the author at donnajunker@roadrunner.com
or any place good books are sold.